"We are all apprentices in a craft no one ever becomes a master."
—Ernest Hemingway

Also by Mark Teppo

Jumpstart Your Novel

The Potemkin Mosaic
Rudolph! He Is the Reason for the Season
The Court of Lies (collection)
Earth Thirst
Heartland
Lightbreaker

THE FOREWORLD SAGA

The Mongoliad (co-authored with Erik Bear, Greg Bear,
Joseph Brassey, Nicole Galland, Cooper
Moo, & Neal Stephenson)
Katabasis (co-authored with Joseph Brassey,
Cooper Moo, & Angus Trim)

The Lion in Chains (co-authored with Angus Trim)
Cimarronin (co-authored with Ellis Amdur,
Charles C. Mann, & Neal Stephenson)

Sinner
Dreamer
Seer
The Beast of Calatrava

PLANNING, PLOTTING, AND PROGRESS

a guide by

MARK
TEPPO

ROTA Books

This is R003, and it has an ISBN of 978-1-63023-100-2.

This book was printed in the United States of America, and it is published by ROTA Books, an imprint of Resurrection House (Puyallup, WA).

Making the words happen

Cover design by Darin Bradley
Cover image by Getty Images, Inc./vicnt
Interior Illustrations by Fran Wilde

First ROTA Books trade paperback edition: March 2016

www.resurrectionhouse.com

PLANNING, PLOTTING, AND PROGRESS

"There is only one plot—things are not what they seem."
—Jim Thompson

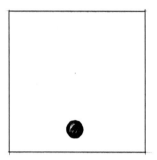

TABLE OF CONTENTS

INTRODUCTION

Writing is hard.

Let's just say that up front, because it's a large part of why we're all here. There's an old saying that "authors" are people who "like to have written," and "writers" are people who "are writing." Writing is, like any other profession, a job that you only get better at by doing. Some have innate talent, which gives them a jump on the rest of us, but mostly, it's dull, dreary work of getting your butt in the chair and yanking words out of your brain.

It's NaNoWriMo as I write this,[1] which happens every year in November, and every year, I use this month as a prompt to get back into the habit of writing on a daily basis. And every year, there are things going on that get in the way of me achieving that goal. Right now, I'm trying to sell my house, and my kids are in a new school, and I'm living at a friend's house in their spare bedroom, which is a twenty-minute drive farther away from where I used to live, and I'm running a small publishing house, which has books coming out now and next year, and I've

---

[1] National Novel Writing Month. It's a frenzied time when every earnest author sits down and tries to crank out the shitty first draft we all have in us. Frankly, we should all do this every month for a year.

got a day job that is filling most of the daylight hours, and, and, and . . .

Where do I write in all this?

The answer is: I don't. I haven't been. I can't figure out where to find the time. Or the energy. Or the enthusiasm. In fact, over the last twelve months, I've written during four of them. Just four.

Good thing I'm writing this book, right?

I get that writing is hard. I really do. There's never enough time. There's never enough quiet head space to do what you need to do in order to write your book. And it's going to be like this for years while you do your time in these nasty trenches of the early days on the road to publication. Someday, the sky will open and angels will descend, bearing down to you the magical certificate that says you have permission from the Universe to give that soul-sucking day job the middle finger and stay home and write full time. And it will be a glorious day, amen. But even then, you'll discover a whole new realm of time-suckers, attention-stealers, and writing obstacles that will keep you from your writing time. Leveling up doesn't make things easier, per se; it just means the obstacles and stressors are different.

This is true of any job, really. You go from working the fryer to microwaving burgers to pushing buttons on the shake machine, and each one of those jobs seems cooler and easier from the other side of the kitchen, but when you get there, you discover they've got their own quirks, which makes the job suck. And even when you get away from the back of the kitchen and can stand at the front and polish the counter between customers, you find out that talking to people is another thing entirely.

This is supposed to be a pep talk, by the way. One of those chatting intros that is supposed to get you all revved up and ready to take on the challenges in this book. Right? Ready to solve your problems and become superstar writers?

The honest secret is that writing is work, and you have to treat it as such. You have to show up—every day—and put in your hours. And if there is no time in the day to put in "hours," then you have to put in minutes. Ten. Fifteen. Twenty. Thirty. Whatever you can get. You have to start somewhere, and you have to keep doing it.

I've been putting off writing down the first part of this book for months, citing the myriad of *more important* things that are on my plate. *I'll get to it tomorrow* has been my daily refrain, and when tomorrow arrives, I say it again. And if you do that too often, *I'll get to it tomorrow* becomes the rule. It becomes your mantra. Your guiding principle. Your default answer.

I'll get to it tomorrow.

Well, it's not what I want carved on my tombstone, frankly. Nor do I want *I wish I had spent more time writing* written there either. So let's make a deal: let's call ourselves "writers," and let's earn that right, okay?

Now, if you haven't started your book, you should go off and do that. At the very least, you might want to grab a copy of Jumpstart Your Novel, and take an hour or two to run through the Nine Box Model method of brain dumping an idea onto the page.[2] When you turn the page in this book, I'm going to assume you've got a book started and that you've reached a point where a) you're stuck, or b) you can't fathom how to find the time to write, or c) you enjoy watching a middle-aged man

---

[2] Shameless plug aside, this is also a warning that I'm going to use some of the lingo and methods from that book under the assumption that you have a passing familiarity with what I'm talking about. So, you know, variable mileage, *caveat elixir*, and all that.

perform cheap circus tricks and make balloon animals. Metaphorically speaking.

These handy icons are going to guide us through the three sections of this book. The first row is the planning row, and we'll spend some time talking about the early stages of writing: organizing your thoughts, building an outline, getting the right beverage (hot or cold), making sure your favorite chair conforms properly to your butt, and finding time to write.

The second row is all about the nuts and bolts and spare parts of the actual novel. How does that outline turn into thousands of words of sparkly prose? How do we get our characters to behave long enough for the story to sweep them away? How do we make a functional plot? How do we make sure we know what we're doing as we write this book?

And finally, with the last row, we'll bring these first two stages together and talk about making it all happen—taking your cocktail-napkin scrawl of an idea to the stack of loose paper filled with illegible "plotting" notes to the last page of your manuscript where you get to type the words "THE END" and go make yourself a strong cocktail. And re-introduce yourself to your family. As an "AUTHOR."[3]

---

[3] Anthony Trollope, who wrote nearly fifty books that were the delight of his generation, never stopped being a "writer." He had an inviolate block of time—three hours a day—where he wrote. If he finished a novel during that block—and no, he didn't start that same novel at the beginning of that block—he would immediately take down a blank sheet of paper and start the next book. So, while there is a great deal of value in rewarding yourself for finishing a project, let's not lose the momentum you've finally built up.

PART ONE

PLANNING

THE ROOT STRUCTURE

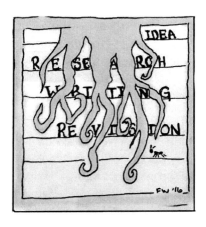

In the beginning, there is an idea. After some time, star stuff and a dust bunny or two stick to the idea, and it becomes something more than a shadow in the darkness. After more time, a chicken bone gets caught, as does a scrap of burlap and maybe some colored string. It's almost an outline! The process gets faster now, like thousands of years of evolution flashing past in a few seconds, like we're caught in a Jan Švankmajer-style stop-motion film. And then the Hand of the Creator writes the magic words—"THE END"—and this odd little bundle of dust and ideas and narrative string is now a book.

Just like that, right?

Well, not quite. The ordering of all these elements is important—they become a structure called "plot,"—and the extra string and dust bunnies and dried-up orange peels get stuck together in little figures that we call "character." The sum is more than the parts, naturally, just as a book is more than merely a random assortment of words strung together. And it's our job as writers to make this weird jangle of plot and character and other shiny parts cohere into something that readers want to take home and treasure forever.

This daunting task is only daunting because you haven't done it a couple hundred times. Writing a book is not unlike learning how to sew or paint an oil portrait or shear a sheep. There are hard ways to accomplish this task, just as there are patterns and tools that make these jobs easier. But, ultimately, what matters is practice. Whether it is using a needle or a brush or a pair of shears or a pen, you get better the more you practice. And when you start out, you work from models and patterns that have been developed by those who have gone before you, until you become proficient enough that you no longer need these guides, and you are ready to strike out on your own.[4]

So, let's start from the beginning with a basic question: what is a book? A book is a story that involves one or more characters who are engaged in a series of events that constitute a narrative arc and that resolves with some manner of internal or external revelation.[5] The book has a beginning, a middle, and an end. Your readers will not appreciate your failure to have each of these three things

---

[4] But you keep these models and patterns handy, right? Because there is a reason these models and patterns persist.

[5] Anyone with a reasonably well-stocked bookcase can, without too much trouble, pluck one or three books from those shelves that don't fit this definition. And that's all fine and good, but I'll argue that each of those books was written by an individual who was consciously forgoing the previous definition because they wanted to say something PURSUANT TO THAT BREAKING OF CONVENTION, and are doing so in full awareness of the definition.

in your book, and it's kind of hard to think of a "finished" book that doesn't have a beginning, middle, and end, but you know what most books lack when they're floating around the writer's head?

The middle.

Everyone knows the beginning of their book. It's usually something like: "Hey, I have this cool idea!" And then you discover your cool idea has an ending. And huzzah! That's usually all we need to start writing. But very quickly, we discover that the distance from "Idea!" to "THE END" can be vast and dark and utterly f*cking unnavigable. This is the bog—the quagmire that lurks at the middle of any book, waiting for any writer not clever enough to escape its suck.

We're going to conquer the bog, and in order to do that, we need to make sure we have a good beginning and a good ending—good infrastructure that will lift us over the endless suck of the bog.

Let's break down "beginning," "middle," and "end" into something a little more useful. In the world of screenwriting, every film is based on a three-act structure. If a film is two hours long, the first act is thirty minutes, the second act is sixty, and the last act is thirty minutes again. If we were to break these acts into chapters, the metric would be 1 to 2 to 1. Five chapters in your first act mean ten chapters in your second and five more in your third.

In my previous book, *Jumpstart Your Novel*, we worked through something called the Nine Box Model in regards to generating a quick outline of your book. It's a series of prompts that take you through a high-level overview of the shape of a book, and it is intended as a means to "jumpstart" an idea into a full-blown book. The nine boxes are arranged in a three-by-three grid, with the first row corresponding to Act 1, the second to Act 2, and the final row to Act 3. Through the exercises in the book, we establish the following sequence for these boxes:

We start with the Protagonist. [BOX 1]
Who is involved in something that Hooks our attention. [BOX 2]
Which reveals the Adversary. [BOX 3]

These three boxes provide enough framework for the author to articulate the Goal of the protagonist. [BOX 4]
In order to achieve this goal, the protagonist suffers a series of Obstacles and Opportunities. [BOX 5] [BOX 6]

While the protagonist is jumping through those hoops, the author considers their Personal Vision for writing this novel. [BOX 7]
Which provides a framework with which to consider the Change the protagonist undergoes during the course of the novel. [BOX 8]
And, ultimately, what has to happen on the page for the author's Personal Goal to be demonstrated via the Change that protagonist undergoes.
Sunset? Field of daisies? Everything goes boom? It all leads to this final resolution. [BOX 9]

Let's start building a chart. We've got the nine boxes and a three-act structure; let's assign a somewhat arbitrary breakdown of eighteen chapters, which isn't quite 1 / 2 / 1, but it's close enough for what we want to accomplish. Again, we're merely making structure at this point. It's going to change as you start getting into the line-by-line of the book, but you can't put in the plumbing for the bathroom until you have the rough shape of the house set up, right?

Let's add a few more narrative structures to this chart. Let's grab Lester Dent's master plot formula,[6] Joseph Campbell's monomyth, and the Celtic Cross style of reading tarot cards. And now our chart—which is going to be your new bestie—looks like the chart on the following page.

Our first icon shows a healthy root structure that is growing down through various strata of compost, sediment, shale, and probably an old dinosaur or two. The first strata of nutrients for your book is the tiny seedling of an idea, which is enough to get you started. But soon thereafter, you hit the layer beneath, and it's not as easy going as that first layer. To help our tiny idea grow into a real book, we need to give it some structure so that it can push through that second layer and reach the third, where the roots start growing every which way.[7]

I'm a fan of research, as well as a fan of buying books that support my *cough* need for research *cough*. But let's avoid overtaxing our already full bookcases with more books that we're probably not going to read quite yet, and spend some time figuring out where this book is going and what shape it is going to take.

---

[6] Once upon a time, Lester Dent wrote a bunch of pulp novels, mostly staring Doc Savage, and as a guide, he developed a Master Plot Formula. It is drafted with a 6,000 word short story in mind, but it still applies to the shape of a novel. You can read the whole thing at paper-dragon.com (http://www.paper-dragon.com/1939/dent.html). What is presented on the chart here is a somewhat cheeky overview meant to suggest a persistent direction to the narrative amongst all the other more academically minded models.

[7] That third layer is where all the visible growth occurs on the surface. Your roots are deep in the "writing" strata, and what is visible up top is lots of major trunk growth and a wild tangle of branches. Don't fret. We'll get to that part soon enough.

CHAPTER	BOX	3-ACT	LESTER DENT	CAMPBELL	TAROT
18	BOX 9			Freedom to Live	THE OUTCOME
17	BOX 8	ACT 3	Resolution	Master of Two Worlds	THE EYE
16				Cross the Return Threshold	THE MIRROR
15	BOX 7			Rescue from Without	
14			Still More Trouble	The Magic Flight	
13	BOX 6			Refusal of Return	THE GUIDE
12		ACT 2		The Ultimate Boon	
11				Apotheosis	
10	BOX 5			Atonement with the Father	
9			More Trouble	Woman as Temptress	
8				Meeting the Goddess	THE VISION
7	BOX 4			The Road of Trials	
6				The Belly of the Whale	
5	BOX 3			The Crossing of the First Threshold	THE OPPOSING FACTOR
4				Supernatural Aid	
3	BOX 2	ACT 1	Heap of Trouble	Refusal of the Call	THE IMMEDIATE FUTURE
2				The Call to Adventure	
1	BOX 1				THE HEART

EXERCISE

Grab yourself a large piece of paper—the larger the better. If you have a roll of art paper or the like and a big table, that'll be perfect. Get a handful of colored pens or pencils, and block out several columns. Let's build a version of the chart that is the shape and structure of your book. We've got our idea, down there at the bottom, right? Let's think about what this book is going to look like as it grows up.

Tick off a number of chapters running up the leftmost side. It's doesn't matter how many, but for the time being, let's consider them as equal sized chapters. I like to map out 5,000 word chapters, and eighteen of them puts me at 90,000 words, which is where I want to end up with my book. Ultimately, I may write twenty-five chapters, because some of those will be shorter than 5,000 words, but at this stage, I'm still thinking at a very high level where there is lots of glossing over the finer details of the plot.[8]

However many chapters you chose, draw a thicker line under the chapter that is the end of Act 1 (25% of your total chapters) and another one under the end of Act 2 (half of your total chapters from this point). If you have an odd number of chapters, like twenty-five, put the extra chapter in Act 2.

If you're familiar with the Nine Box Model from *Jumpstart Your Novel*, fill in the corresponding boxes in a separate column with your own notes. If not, just put some shorthand notes from the description above in these boxes.

You can write in the Dent variants of "And then things

---

[8] In the case of 25 chapters, we'd have 6 in Act 1, 13 in Act 2, and 6 in Act 3.

get worse" in a third column, or you can merely drop in an increasingly greater number of upward pointing arrows.

That'll leave us with two more columns: one for the mythic hand-waving and the other one for the mystic "shit"—you know, the good stuff that you mix in with the dirt to help your tree grow strong and tall.[9]

---

[9] Speaking of good shit in your soil, you should read the chapter in Charles C. Mann's *1491* that talks about the soil in the Amazon and what it was like before those pesky Europeans showed up.

THE MYTHS OF THE MYTH

Joseph Campbell gets a lot of grief about getting all reductionist on the vast wealth of the cultural mythologies throughout the world, but what his seminal book, *The Hero With a Thousand Faces*, did was enumerate the fundamental similarities among many of these disparate stories. It was never a lesson in "this is the one true way to tell a story." Rather, Campbell was taking stock and recognizing that many of the stories of the human condition follow a common arc, regardless of language or locale or cultural make-up. The arc of the hero—the protagonist in our story—has a distinct shape.

As writers, it is important for us to know the natural rhythm of a story because this is what makes our audiences get that warm, tingling feeling in their bellies. It's what is going to make them show up again and again for more stories. Long-running television shows or book series don't run long because they're constantly changing their shape. They run long because they are comfortable in their familiarity.

Recently, a bestselling suspense writer offered the statistic that a vast majority of the American reading public only buys two books a year, and one of those books is bought in an airport bookstore.[10] I was, at the time I read this bit of data, reading both this author's first book and his current book (somewhere near the two-dozen mark in the series), and one of the noticeable differences in the author's style between those two books was the lack of words on the page in the current book. And it occurred to me that most flights are three to four hours long, and if you're buying a book in an airport, you're looking for something to entertain you for only three to four hours.

Familiarity does not breed contempt. Familiarity breeds an open wallet.

Know the rhythms of story. Know the traditional structures. They will guide you, especially when you're in the early stages of planning a narrative arc. You can go off-structure later, but do it when you know where you want to go and why. We all hate the axiom of "Know the rules before you break them" because it means that we have to follow the rules first, and following the rules is always a pain in the ass, right? How many of you read all the instructions that come with your new electronic gizmo before you start using it?[11]

Uh huh. That's what I thought.

Anyway, Campbell gave us a simple chart that breaks down the natural rhythm of a narrative arc. It doesn't work for every story that you might want to tell, but it will work for a vast majority of them. If your book feels

---

[10] I'm not going to cite the conversation because the author didn't explicitly offer his source for this data, because if it is true, then it means that you and I and all our friends are doing a lot to sway the statistics every time we buy a book somewhere else. Like, you know, daily. Which is groovy of us, but it still makes me sad. The validity of this data point is also outside the scope of my anecdote so just roll with it, okay?

[11] Notice how most gizmos don't even come with instructions any more. They come with tips and help files and other things that get in the way of using the gizmo for a period of time. Because that's the only way you'll bother to pay attention to the instructions for the gizmo's feature set.

like you're trying to shove a Spandex body stocking onto an overweight, gassy goat, it's probably because you're trying to be clever and dress the goat from the back end first. And that's just the wrong way to dress a goat.[12]

The Hero's Journey is cyclical. In the simplest description, it is the story of a protagonist who must leave their safe and predictable life and embark upon a perilous journey. The journey takes them to a world unlike the one they know, and upon their return, they have been transformed by their journey, which allows them to return to their normal lives, but with one difference. Usually a pretty big one.[13]

The chart we've got runs down the list of Campbell's various stages of the Hero's Journey, and it's a rare story that actually hits every single stage. I've listed them all merely to give you a number of places where you can hook in your narrative. Not every story has to have a Meeting with the Goddess, a trial of Woman as Temptress, a little Atonement with the Father, AND some Apotheosis. Unless you're working on a doorstopper of an epic coming-of-age fantasy sequence that spans eighteen volumes, in which case, each of those is a single volume. More likely, your story will have a confrontation between the protagonist and some aspect of themselves in the alternate world, typically either a confrontation

---

[12] And no, and I'm not buying that your plan is "symbolic of the worker's plight under the weight of a bloated oligarchy, wherein the members of the oligarchy revel in shitting on those who support their oppressive social and momentary constructs." Basically, because I know there is no model there for a long-running series.

[13] There are a number of books out there that distill the Hero's Journey down to various prompts and life-affirming examples, but really, if you're interested in the minutia of Campbell's research, just go get a copy of *The Hero With a Thousand Faces*. Yes, it can get dense in its minutia, but Campbell came back to the book several times during his career, and his final edition in 2008 does some nice summary work that is invaluable to the writer brain.

with the familial figure opposite them or a reconciliation with that familial guide whom they have been seeking.

In *Star Wars*, for instance, we can read Vader killing Ben Kenobi as a removal of the possibility of atonement with the Father (Ben, who was a surrogate father for Luke), which galvanizes Luke to embrace his destiny (enlightened ghost Ben even tells him as much later on). Or the scene can be read as Ben sacrificing himself to Vader in order to show Luke the true power of the Force, which is an apotheosis of the magi figure that allows the protagonist to see the path they must take in order to realize their full potential. Or, Vader—who is Luke's actual father—kills the false father, Ben Kenobi, in an attempt to reconcile himself with his absent son. You can read it any number of ways, but the actual action of that scene remains the same.[14]

And not all protagonists pass through all the stages in the same fashion. For instance, while Luke laments that he'll never get off the rock that is Tatooine (and doesn't, in fact, until he is spirited away by the wise magi, Ben Kenobi), which is representative of the "refusal of the call" stage, in *The Hunger Games*, Katniss Everdeen volunteers for the games to protect her sister. Her "call to adventure" is a threat against her family, and she bypasses the "refusal of the call" altogether.

Many of the myths that Campbell investigated are patriarchal in design, and the protagonist is typically male. It

---

[14] Now, I'll bet that Lucas didn't know that Vader was Luke's father at the time *Star Wars* was written and filmed, but the fact that the revelation at the end of *Empire* doesn't negate the power of Kenobi's death scene speaks to the effectiveness of the underlying mythological arc that Lucas clung to for *Star Wars*. In fact, knowing the true lineage between the characters actually makes that scene in *Star Wars* work more effectively because of how it fits into the mythological structure, and why the sequence in *The Empire Strikes Back* where Luke confronts the phantasm of his father on Dagobah and fails is a secondary repetition of the protagonist's cycle through this journey.

doesn't mean that all narrative is bound to this structure. Campbell was outlining a specific type of narrative structure found throughout different cultures, and understandably, in an effort to buttress his thesis, his emphasis was on data that supported the conclusion he was seeking. The structural nature of the Hero's Journey—as well as the cultural foundations these myths supported—was based on the fact that the role of protector and hero was a male role. The shape of the narrative arc is defined by the traditional male role in society, but that does not negate the entirety of the mythological structure for women—especially women in a modern society that does not have the same strictly defined roles for men and women.

And these differences also shape the protagonist's arcs. There's an underlying whiff of revenge in Luke's arc (the Empire did kill his adopted parents, after all), and because violence has been done to him, he is allowed do violence in return. Katniss, on the other hand, is protecting her family, who have been threatened with violence. Her refusal, if she has one, is her reluctance to do violence to others, until it is absolutely necessary.[15] It can be argued that her use of violence is driven by revenge as well, but ask yourself: did Luke ever pass up the opportunity to kill a stormtrooper when he had the chance?

Once the protagonist leaves the safety of their home (the world they knew), they must journey to a gate where they must face a gatekeeper. Once they pass the gate, they enter a sacred space where the rules of the normal world are suspended.[16] Various adventures occur here, culmi-

---

[15] Notice that during the first game, she becomes the mother figure to Rue, signifying her own transformation from child to woman. This is her Meeting with the Goddess moment, and she does not need the other stages to accomplish her goal.

[16] Mircea Eliade calls this "sacred" space in contrast with the "profane" space of the normal world (cf., The Sacred and The Profane).

nating in an event that transforms the hero, whereupon the journey back home begins. If we imagine the cycle as a circle, it might look something like the following:

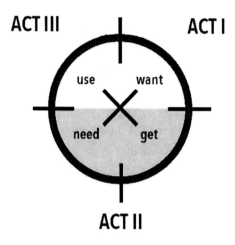

Notice how the crossing of the gate into the sacred world and the return to profane space coincide with the separation between acts? Act I defines the world of the narrative for us, and the break between Act I and Act II is a change in the world as it has been defined. It's not merely an awareness of the threat that faces the protagonist and their world; it is a shift into the unknown. In *The Hunger Games*, it happens in that moment when Katniss steps into the arena where the games are fought. In *Star Wars*, it happens when Han Solo triggers the hyperdrive and the stars get all streaky and the Millennium Falcon vanishes from the screen.[17]

You will get some compression of the journey once the hero has been transformed. It's like getting a bonus

---

[17] And then they get swallowed by the giant space whale, er, Death Star.

coupon for leveling up. Once the hero has received the boon they sought to receive in sacred space, they are afforded certain privileges on their return. Cynically, we can look upon these privileges as narrative short-hand. While the journey to the nadir of the circle is well-documented as the series of obstacles and opportunities that test and refine the character of the protagonist, the return is shortened for several reasons. Primarily, the protagonist has received their boon and/or been enlightened, and there is no longer a need to document their struggle because the bulk of their struggle (which has been a quest for identity as well) is over. What remains is merely an application of their newfound knowledge to the greater crisis facing their profane world.

And secondly, your audience has been patient. Once they know the hero has the goods, they want to see the ultimate showdown. As writers, it's best not to make them wait too long.

This is why the eagles show up really late in *The Lord of the Rings*. It's not until Frodo and Sam have gone through the crucible and been reformed that they are allowed to use their Post-Transformation Voucher.[18] Yes, the book would have been much shorter if the eagles had just come and picked everyone up at Rivendell back in the beginning, but the heroes had not suffered through their journey into the mythic space yet. You don't get the coupon without singeing some hair and losing a pair of pants or two. But, once you get your Post-Transformation Voucher, then yes, it's straight to the top of the queue for you.

The hero—transformed, enlightened, recipient of the boon of the Goddess—returns to their home, and in

---

[18] Frodo has lost everything but the Ring during his passage through Cirith Ungol and the lair of Shelob, right? He's basically naked on the plain of fire.

some climatic encounter, vanquishes the Adversary, thereby saving their community. Huzzah!

Note that it is not uncommon for the hero to then leave their community. Not because they've seen the world and are now bored with the mundanity of living at home again, but because they have been transformed. If they have done violence during the course of their journey, then they are marked with that blood. They are, in some ways, dangerous to their community. They cannot stay because they imperil the innocents.[19]

EXERCISE

Draw a circle on the page beneath your chart. Quarter it like the illustration above. Write the chapter number that represents that break between the Acts (at ninety degree increments). Put hash marks along the circle for the remaining chapters. Working clockwise around your circle, write the words "WANT," "GET," "NEED," and "USE" in each quadrant. Consider how these words reflect the course of the narrative in each section. Notice the subtle distinctions between "WANT" and "NEED" and "GET" and "USE," and how each pair is opposite each other on the circle. "WANT" is in profane space; "NEED" is in sacred space. Both are emotional drivers for the story. "GET" and "USE" are applications of the prior sections' emotional impetus.

---

[19] See William Munny in Clint Eastwood's *Unforgiven*. He constantly warns the kid of the dangers of hiring a killer, and sure enough, things get out of hand.

USING COMPOST

I like Tarot decks.[20] I have more than I can reasonably hold, and I use them regularly when I'm working on a book. I am, if it isn't already abundantly clear, a pantser—a writer who likes to write by the seat of their pants. I do draw up outlines, and I do a lot of thinking (but probably not enough planning), but over the years, I've come to realize that if I overplan a book, then all of the magic goes out of the writing for me. I'm not excited about what's going onto the page, and I'm pretty sure my boredom translates right to the reader. Therefore, I write

---

[20] No one has really put forth a definitive history of the tarot, but it is generally accepted that the cards came to Western Europe via Mameluke soldiers who played a card game with disks, swords, staves, and cups as suits. During the Middle Ages, this game became all the rage in Italy, and as it moved north and west, it started to pick up regional flavor. But it wasn't really until the esoteric revival in France and England during the 18th and 19th centuries that the deck grew to its current size of seventy-eight cards. Fifty six are the Minor Arcana, the suit cards that we know from modern playing cards with one additional court card; the remaining twenty-two are the Major Arcana, the highly symbolic portion of the deck that is more widely known when folks chat about Tarot, like they do.

Actually, my favorite "history" of the tarot is one put forth by Barth Anderson in his novel, *The Magician and the Fool*. Trust a writer to come up with a delightfully outlandish explanation for the holes in history.

to be amazed by what the characters want to do, which is a bit of a dangerous way to write. It can turn really unproductive as you and the characters wrestle with what the book is about, but once everyone gets on the same page, the work happens quickly.

One of the ways I plan is to feed my subconscious.

The subconscious brain is really good at untangling knots and figuring out pathways through mazes—especially when you're not paying attention to it. Your brain is always working on some issue with the book, whether you're aware of it or not, and when it has a problem solved, it'll shove the solution into your conscious mind.

To that end, Tarot is a great way to stick a bunch of archetypal symbols and concepts into your subconscious brain, which will happily chew on them for food as it works through the puzzles and mazes. The cards are rarely literal and are meant to be suggestive. You have to provide a narrative to their arrangement on the table. You have to tell a story, basically, and in doing so, I've found that aspects of the book I'm working on become more clear, mainly because I've had to articulate some unexpected pathway though the narrative that has been suggested by the cards (and picked up and applied by my subconscious mind).

And if you throw down a spread, and it makes absolutely no sense in regard to your plot or your characters, by all means, pick the cards up and try again. The tarot should open up options that you hadn't previously considered or hadn't noticed. They don't force a structure that is contrary to the writer's desire.

When I do a Jumpstart Your Novel workshop, I always bring a deck of tarot cards with me, and I tell the class that I'll draw a card for anyone who gets stuck on one of the questions in the exercises we're doing. Typically, the class is skeptical of this sort of madness. However, more often than not, every card drawn is a surprise and a revelation to the writer. It's a lot of fun to watch their faces light up as if I'm doing some fabulous magic trick by providing them the exact visual cue they needed in order to cut through the knot they had been fighting.

The cards aren't magic. It's our ability to instinctively see patterns and create narrative that is.

There are many ways to do a reading with the tarot, but I have found that the Celtic Cross style of reading matches up nicely with the chart we're building for our book. Before you start the reading, focus your mind on a question you want some insight into—or, in the case of our outline, a narrative arc for a protagonist. The tarot deck is divided into two major portions: the Minor Arcana, suit cards; and the Major Arcana, twenty-two cards that are larger archetypes. I tend to do these readings using only the Major Arcana cards, because I find their meaning and symbolisms speak more directly to the thematic arc. The Minor Arcana are fine, but they tend to reference elements and events on a smaller scale.[21]

However you decide to do your reading, lay out ten cards in a pattern that resembles a cross and a staff (six on the left, four on the right—see the previous image). Each position in the Cross has a specific meaning that we'll map to our narrative arc.[22]

---

[21] Compare the Six of Swords which means "a regretful but necessary transition" and The Tower, which depicts a bolt of lightning striking a tower and hurling a couple of crown-wearing unfortunates into the void. The former sounds like a minor inconvenience; the latter is an "OMG! We're all going to die!" sort of event. Which one is going to have a more dramatic impact on the narrative shape of your novel?

[22] Refer to Appendix B for an example reading.

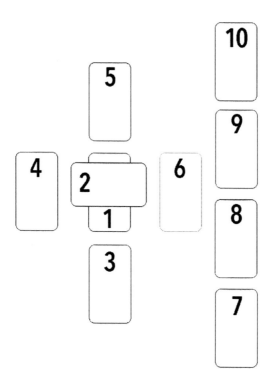

1. THE HEART OF THE MATTER.

This card represents the protagonist. It can be a literal representation. It can be an occupational representation. This is how the author refers to the protagonist. It may not strictly be their job or their identity. For instance, any character played by Will Ferrell in a film could readily be represented by The Fool card, and what changes from film to film is merely the character's occupation and situation. We'll still think of him as a bumbling well-meaning idiot, or, like we see in many decks, the buffoon who is unaware that he's about to walk off a cliff or that a dog wants to snack on his nutsack.

2. THE OPPOSING FACTOR.

This is the complicating factor that disguises or otherwise obscures the Heart (which is why it is laid at a ninety degree angle across the first card). Think of this card as the Adversary, aka "that which opposes the protagonist." In narratives that force that protagonist to deal with the natural world (any Jack London story, for instance), the opposition comes from the natural world.

In *San Andreas*, one of the most recent natural disaster morality films, Dwayne Johnson AKA The Rock is opposed by a great earthquake that tries to drop the grand state of California into the Pacific Ocean. Characters who get in his way certainly qualify as antagonists, but they are more properly categorized as either agents of the Adversary or as obstacles that our heroic protagonist must overcome in order to win against the Adversary.

Some Tarot cards don't explicitly represent people. For instance, it can be hard to look at The Moon, which represents the divine creative madness that either liberates or destroys, and immediately think, "Oh, yes, this is Biff, the protagonist's childhood nemesis who has gone on to become a megalomaniacal industrialist who has never forgotten (or forgiven) that wedgie the protagonist gave him during gym one day in high school, and now, twenty years later, has built an entire chemical weapons manufacturing empire just so that he can dose the water supply of the small town where the protagonist lives merely for petty REVENGE!"[23]

---

[23] It only seems petty to the protagonist, of course. For Biff, this has been an all-consuming fixation for many, many years, and the protagonist's seeming unawareness of Biff's long-standing rage and embarrassment only increases how horrifically everyone the protagonist ever loved is going to die after drinking the tainted water. Especially the innocent children of the orphanage where Biff works.

Don't worry some much about the literal interpretation of the card, and let a more symbolic apsect of the card suggest the nature of the Adversary to you. Ask and answer the question of why does this card oppose the protagonist?

3. THE ROOTS.

There is a foundation beneath the protagonist, even if they have been shoved out of their comfort zone. Who were they? Where did they come from? Who supported them in the past and why? You'll notice that both this card and the next don't show up on the chart, and that's because they are beneath and behind the protagonist. This is character depth, if you will.

4. THE PAST.

That which is immediately behind the protagonist. As noted above, this card isn't on the chart because it is behind the protagonist. Now, we can certainly backfill some of the protagonist's history into the narrative, but only at the service of the narrative. Your readers aren't going to care about a huge chunk of backstory if they don't know anything about who the protagonist is and what they are doing first.

Richard Stark wrote a series of books about a thief named Parker. One of the clever things he did was that he set the narrative viewpoint as third party limited whenever Parker was the focus of the story. We never get to know what goes on Parker's head, which means his backstory is always hidden from us.

At the beginning of the first book, *The Hunter*, Parker is walking across the George Washington Bridge into New York City. We see that he's a bastard and that he's on a mission, but we don't know why. Stark keeps the narrative moving forward—Parker gets to the city, Parker reinvents himself, Parker finds Lynn (his ex-wife), he threatens her about the whereabouts of someone named Mal—without giving the audience a chance to really ground themselves. And it's not until we learn about the existence of Mal that Stark takes a break and gives us enough backstory to make us happy.

Contrast this with the 1967 movie version called *Point Blank*,[24] which begins with ten minutes of incomprehensibly chaotic backstory shoved at the viewers while "Walker"[25] lies in a jail cell in Alcatraz. By the time we get to the walking across the bridge scene (rendered in the film as Marvin's character walking through LAX), we've been given all of the backstory that Stark keeps from us, and the problem with this version is that we've been confused by too many disconnected elements and the fact that Walker comes across as a drunk rube who gets taken advantage of by both Mal and some dude who apparently works for the FBI when he's not riding the tour boat across San Francisco Bay.

In *The Hunter*, we know there is history to these characters, and it informs how and why they interact in the narrative arc of the novel, but we don't see it until we need it.

Kurt Vonnegut once offered eight rules of writing.[26] The eighth rule says: "Give your readers as much information as possible as soon as possible."

---

[24] One of John Boorman's first features, and a major starring role for Lee Marvin. Too bad it's also part of the brightly lit New Wave period of noir in film. I blame Godard and the Dave Clark 5.

[25] Why they couldn't name him "Parker" is beyond me. The same is true for *Payback*, the Mel Gibson version, where the protagonist is "Porter." It's like some studio exec somewhere laid down a mandate that the studio was doing their own version (even though they gave Stark a "Based on" credit). In which case, the name would be different, like "Horker" or "Tucker."

[26] See the prefatory remarks to his 1999 collection, *Bagombo Snuff Box*.

I have a caveat: "Give this information only when the readers are ready to understand what it means."

Stark strings us along for two chapters before he gives us any of this history, and he knows that he's testing our patience, which is why the book cooks right along until that point. We'll give him some leeway, but eventually we're going to want some backstory, and just before we're about to lose our patience with him, he gives us what we want. And we're eager for it because we know we need it![27]

5. THE ALTERNATE FUTURE (AKA THE VISION).

This is the future the protagonist seeks—their goal, their idealized realized state of being. Who they want to be, if you will, but it can also be read as the world they want to live in.

This is the vision that drives the protagonist to step out of their normal—read safe—world and embark upon their journey. They want something, which forces them to make a change (or the change is forced upon them, in which case what they want may very well be a means or tool that will allow them to return to their preferred state of rest).

"As above, so below" is an old alchemical saying that is the key to the mystical transformation of both metals and men, meaning that transformations in both metaphysical and spiritual states can (and should) be mirrored in

---

[27] *Point Blank* makes us watch Lee Marvin hang out at Alcatraz (which is abandoned at this time) while he magically heals from several gunshot wounds. All the while, we're scratching our heads and wondering why he's hanging off the barbed wire fence like's just some dude catching rays. Contrast again with *Payback*, Brian Helgeland's studio-mangled remake. The studio slapped a voice-over driven intro that basically boils down *Point Blank*'s extended opening to about a minute and a half. The voice-over totally puts us in protagonist's head, but it also immediately grounds us, which is good because we've paid $10 for the seat and another $10 for a tub of popcorn, and we're not sitting in the dark theater to be confused by a narrative we have to think through.

physical states as well. The card above the protagonist and the card below the protagonist (3: THE ROOT) are tied together in that the protagonist is supported by one as they reach for the other. Or that influences in one mirror change in the other. There is a cyclical structure to the protagonist's life that circles down from the VISION to the HEART to the ROOT to the HEART to the VISION again, and each state change carries with it influence from the card it has just passed through.

This is readily seen in the old vegetation cult rituals where a young man is elevated to being "king" of the tribe. After a year, he is removed from office (typically sacrificed—in a manner just as you might expect), the tribe goes through a period of mourning, and then a new king is elected, returning the tribe to the elevated VISION state again.

6. THE IMMEDIATE FUTURE.

That which is immediately before the protagonist. Even though the previous five cards inform who the protagonist is, what is most pressing is what is happening RIGHT NOW.

In the narrative structure, this is mapped to the events that are occurring at the opening of the book. In any Clive Cussler novel (or James Bond film, for that matter), we are always treated to a short sequence wherein our protagonist (Dirk Pirk or James Bond) is in the midst of some dangerous assignment (though, in Dirk's case, more often than not, he's just out diving for treasure when nefarious hirelings start shooting at him). This is typically the "before credits" sequence in a film where our attention becomes transfixed by what is going on, and it may very well play into the larger narrative arc that is the full story, but it is a stand-alone sequence that exists mainly to introduce us to the world and the protagonist.

If we look at the physical layout of the cards on the table, there is a straight line from the protagonist's past to his identity (obscured slightly by the adversary) to the immediate future. Think of Parker walking across the George Washington Bridge. He's moving in a straight line, walking from the past to the future, his eyes on his destination. This is how we approach the opening of the narrative: a straight line to the immediate future with our protagonist.

7. THE MIRROR.

This is typically representative of how the querent sees themselves: their identity, when everything is stripped away.

For the author, this drifts outside the direct scope of the narrative, in a way. Regardless of whether we explicitly reveal who the protagonist truly is, we have to give our readers some measure of this revelation, and how much we want to give them and in what manner we want to reveal this secret about our protagonist speaks to how we're going to approach the book. Stark wanted to explore the anti-hero with Parker, but he didn't want to get lost in the psychology of the "villain," so he kept us removed from Parker. But that doesn't stop us from knowing *who* Parker is. We just don't know the *why*, but that's the story that Stark wanted to tell.

So, while the MIRROR is representative of the protagonist, it is also a reflection of us as the writer.

8. THE EYE.

How the outsider world perceives the protagonist.

This is part of the source of the conflict within the book. Who the protagonist thinks they are and how they are perceived by the rest the world are not in sync. This misperception is what forces the protagonist out of their comfort zone. It is what starts them on the course of the narrative arc. Additionally, how they are going to deal with this external perception informs both their internal narrative arc (see the MIRROR above) and their external arc.

This card underlies a big chunk of the second act of the book. This is where the struggle lies. And isn't that always the case with figuring out how to make the rest of the world see us as we really are? Your poor characters are no different. Always misunderstood.

9. THE GUIDE.

The guide shows that path that leads from the HEART to the MIRROR through the VISION and the EYE. More concretely, this is a suggestion for the obstacles and opportunities that are presented to the protagonist over the course of the narrative. Is the path to the goal straight-forward or complicated? Is it simple or Byzantine in construction?

For Parker, in *The Hunter*, it was the simplest of paths: he simply kept going to the next guy up the food chain within the Outfit, explaining how Mal owed him money, and since Mal gave that money to the Outfit, the Outfit now owed Parker. The Outfit didn't quite see it that way, and therein lies the central conflict of the novel.

Now, *Game of Thrones* or *War or Peace* are a little more complicated . . .

10. THE OUTCOME.

Regardless of who the protagonist thinks they are or who they think they are going to become, there is an ultimate transformation or resolution to their journey, which is represented by this final card. Does the author respect the protagonist's wishes and realize their VISION or is the final scene in the novel a different resolution entirely? What is the authorial intent in this ending? How does that change our understanding of the protagonist's journey? Is their journey complete?

In most serial narratives (i.e., television shows or long-running book series), the characters reset themselves at the end of the novel. They may change or grow over the course of the arc, but they remain fundamentally the same, and this is the natural inclination of such fiction. The lesson imparted though the narrative arc is meant for the reader and not necessarily for the protagonist.[28]

EXERCISE

You know how this works. Grab a deck. Lay out the cards. Walk through the commentary above as you analyze each card in reference to your outline. Scribble notes that reference each card in the respective area of your chart.

Again, and I really want to stress this, if all of this seems like mystical bullshit, skip it. Doing a reading like this—at this stage in the planning process—is not a substitute for knowing your narrative arc. It is meant to amplify what you already have in mind. The cards merely remind you that your subconscious has your back. This is a tool that you can reference later when you get caught in the Dark Well of Despair—a knotted rope, if you will, that you can used to climb out of the well.

---

[28] Fortunately, we've moved past needing those final moments where everyone sits around and gabs about the After School Special moment that's been loaded into the final act of the narrative. Whew.

THE ENDLESS LIST

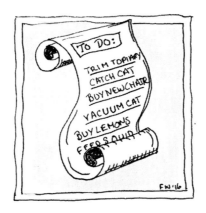

Okay, so now we have a bunch of notes scrawled across a large piece of paper. Look at that! The book is right there! We're done, right?

Alas, no.

We know what the book looks like. We know its structure, and we have a reasonable sense of what has to happen in what order. But the actual parade of words across the page—all eighty or ninety or a hundred thousand of them—still has to be done. And if you're like me, you have no idea where you're going to find the time to actually do all this work. In fact, having built this chart probably drives home the point that you really don't know when or how you're going to finish this book. Which is completely understandable. What you've got on the page in front of you is a LOT of work, and some of it is probably still completely vague and filled with magical hand-waving with a liberal application of mystical "shit."

"OMG, it's not a book!" you wail. "Damn you, Teppo! You lied to me. It's just more notes!"

Hold on, there, Skippy. Actually, you've just built a roadmap. A process chart that tells you exactly what happens, and in what order. The trick now is to figure out how to turn this roadmap into actual words. To accomplish that, we need to get our butts in our chairs and get some writing done, which means we should talk about time management.

Oh, managing time. First, we invent the whole concept, and then we turn around and create an entire industry devoted to teaching you how to better manage this artificial construct we invented in the first place. Weren't our lives easier before we got all this high-tech awareness of the eternal half-life decay of the cesium atom? Back when we were all preternaturally young and beautiful and lived stress free lives down by the water.

But, alas, we can't undo this awareness, and so we have become both the keepers of time and the wasters of time. What we have to do is learn to focus on the former and stop celebrating being the latter. There are many other books out there that will inveigle you for hundreds of pages about time management and list management and all those other aspects of personal management that will make you a highly productive, whirlwind self-manager, and you should certainly avail yourself of one (or all) of those books if you'd like to explore these topics more fully. We're here to talk about writing, so we'll only dally for a short while on the topic of time management. We'll keep it simple, and then we'll get into a modicum of math and earnest aphorisms.

Time, for all of its metaphysical and philosophical ephemerality, has a very real presence in our lives. We treat it as if it were a quantifiable object. "I don't have time for this," we say. "How much time is this meeting going to take?" "When was the last time you bathed?" We have watches and clocks and floating displays on our computer screens that constantly remind us of the passage of time. And we always moan about not having enough.

Enough of what? If we substituted "jelly beans" for "time" in the previous sentences, you'd think I was spouting nonsense. "I don't have the jelly beans for this." What does that even mean? I don't have the requisite amount of some sort of currency to afford whatever "this" is? Well, if we're talking jelly beans, I could go get some more, right? But if we're talking about time, where do I get more of it? I can't, can I?

But why not?

Now, let's get to the subject of to-do lists. These lists range from grocery lists to complex Gantt project management charts, and the fundamental unit of each and every list is the line item. A grocery list—"bread," "milk," eggs," "spatula," "cat food"—is a list of items that you need to acquire at the grocery store. This list is a subset of another list, the "Things To Do Before I Go Home" list. By going to the grocery store and getting each of those five items, I get to check off "go to grocery store" from my other list. And while I am at the store, I can only get one of those items at a time.

This is really important: you can only do one line item on any list at any given time.

Now, someone will pipe up from the back about multi-tasking and efficiency models and all that, and yes, that's what all those other time management books are all about. Regardless of what those earnest tomes tell you about multitasking and split brain efficiency, you are still only doing one thing at any given moment. If our lives were Gantt charts, "go to the grocery store" would be an item with multiple dependencies, a secondary list that is zipped up beneath this top-level item—"get bread," "get milk," "get eggs," "get spatula for secret nighttime project," "get food for that small mammal that makes that funny noise at night." We're being efficient by grouping these items under "go to the grocery store," but fundamentally, while we were walking up and down the aisle at the store, searching for bread, we were not also searching for spatulas. Maybe we'll pass the spatulas, and think: "Oh hey, spatulas! That's on my list." And we'll re-order our processes to chose a spatula, check it off our list, and continue our search for bread.

A to-do list is a simple structure. Each item is listed on a single line. *I'm going to do X, and then I'm going to do Y, and after that, I'll do Z.* Sure, multitasking may let you do X and Y and Z all at once, but let's be kind to ourselves here and insist that we only write one chapter at a time, okay? Because this is an important part of time management in creative work. You have to focus on the task in front of you, and there can only be one task.

You could look at your list of chapters and treat them like looking for bread and finding spatulas in the store, but chapters in a book aren't quite the same line item. Unlike bread and spatulas, chapters have an internal dependency built in. They are listed in order because that is part of the narrative arc of the book. I know people who write their chapters out of order—they hop from scene to scene, and this makes me crazy, by the way—and there's certainly nothing wrong with writing a book this

40

way IF IT WORKS FOR YOU. The important thing here is to recognize that each chapter is a distinct item on your list, and in order to complete the list, you have to check off each chapter as an individual unit.[29]

I'm being pedantic here to make a point, so bear with me for a little bit. A chapter is a line item on your list of to-dos. It is a collection of words that you acknowledge as a required unit of the overall book. As I mentioned previously, I like to work with eighteen chapters, and I arbitrarily assign 5,000 words to each chapter so that I end up with a 90,000 word book. Modify this to whatever length and requirement you have for your book, but there is a quantifiable number of words that will fit in each chapter.

Now, ask yourself how fast do you write? I tend to clock in at about a 1,000 words an hour, and this is a "rough draft, banging on the keyboard and making the words appear" sort of pace. Which means, roughly speaking, it'll take me ninety hours to write a draft of this book. It'll take me five hours to finish a chapter.

The act of writing a book is a math problem. How fast do you write times (rate/hour) times number of words in the book (length) equals number of hours required to write the book. In other words:

$$length / rate = hours$$

Using the numbers I provided earlier, it'll take me ninety hours to write this book. If I write an hour a day, five days a week, it'll take me eighteen weeks to write this book—four and a half months. If I did that on a regular schedule, I would finish three books a year. If I wrote

---

[29] You can, of course, break each chapter down into distinct sub-lists—individual scenes, perhaps—which make them more like grocery items subordinate to a grocery task line item. You have to complete all of the subordinate line items in order to check off the primary item.

seven days a week, it'd shave a month off that time. In other words, I could write another book during the year if I spent two hours writing every weekend. Two hours!

From a purely mathematical standpoint, there are 8,760 hours in a year. Even if you stare at the ceiling for a third of them and work at a full-time job for another third, there are still almost 3,000 hours every year that are not taken up with sleeping and being an office drone. I'm not trying to make you feel bad about your time management skills or pass judgement on how busy your life is; I'm just noting that the amount of time it takes to get your butt in the chair and write a book is less than 5% of the available hours in a given year.

So why is that 5% so hard to find?

Well, there's a couple hundred thousand reasons, and many of them are completely valid, but a lot of them also fall into the broad category of Spurious Time Suckage. Let's sidestep talking about SPS for a moment and focus on GWT—Glorious Writing Time. How do we find these magical units of GWT in order to write our book?

EXERCISE

Do the math for your book. How fast do you write? How long is your book? How many hours will it take for you finish a draft?

Look at your schedule for any given day. How many hours do you sleep? How many hours do you work? How much commuting time is there? How long does it take you to cram a piece of toast in your mouth in the morning while you try to find a clean outfit? How long does it take to reheat dubious looking leftovers from last week at night? Do you go to the gym, and if so, for how long?

How many hours are left?

Multiply that by .05.

Given your current schedule, this is the amount of time (in fractions of an hour) that you can reasonably allocate to writing. If you have four hours a day that aren't otherwise allocated, then 5% of those four hours is twelve minutes. That is your minimum daily GWT. At one thousand words an hour, you can write 200 words in those twelve minutes, and it will take you one year and three months to write your book.

Of course, this minimum is unacceptable, right? We'd like to be writing more, and so let's get our butts in our chairs and figure out how improve our unit of GWT.

BUTT IN CHAIR

The singular secret to writing is putting your butt in a chair and writing. It doesn't matter if you use a laptop/desktop/tablet/Etch-a-Sketch. It doesn't matter if you write longhand with a pencil/pen/crayon/silver-tipped stylus dipped in blood. All that matters is that words get out of your brain and onto the page. As we discussed in the last chapter, the book happens because you make the words. Nothing else matters. That's the simplest rule of the universe. You write, therefore, the book gets finished.

Previously, we established a unit that we called Glorious Writing Time—the GWT. The time it takes to write a book is measured in a set number of GWTs, and what differs from writer to writer (and book to book, for that matter), is the actual length of each unit of GWT in real world minutes. If you're ultra-busy every single minute of every single day, and your GWT is only twelve minutes, then it's going to take you a little while to write 100,000 words. If your GWT is four hours, then we all expect you to have that book finished by Thursday. It's all relative, and there is no correct answer other than knowing the length of time that is one unit of GWT.

This is your basic bargaining chip with the universe.

In fact, I would recommend buying a set of poker chips. You can get them at nearly any store that has a toy section. Whatever color they have the most of is your single unit of GWT. Let's say these are the red chips. Blue chips are worth five red ones. Green are worth five blue. Black are worth five green. Now that you have these chips, you have to negotiate with the universe for how they are going to be used. And everyone will have a different situation in their life. Regardless, the chips make things real. Your support structure understands these tokens more readily than they do the nebulous argument that you have to "go write."[30]

For instance, recently, we decided not to put my kids in the summer all-day care program (to their delight), which was going to be a problem for my productivity when a constant parade of squealing children going up and down the stairs was going to happen ALL DAY LONG. I called the kids into my office and showed them a bunch of cards with various prizes written on them. I put the cards in a box, and told them that for every blue chip they earned, they'd get to draw from the hat.

"How do we get blue chips?" they asked.

"You earn five red chips," I said.

---

[30] To them, "writing" is you staring at a computer screen for an hour and bitching at them for interrupting you, when all they see you doing is trying to hide the fact that you're playing some Facebook game. This gets a little hard to justify.

"And how do we get red ones?" they asked.

"For every half hour I get of uninterrupted time, you earn a red chip," I said. "If you solve a conflict between yourselves over who poked who first without yelling 'Dad!,' you get a red chip. If you can manage to not slam the front door during the endless to and fro-ing, you get a chip. Got it?"

They got it, and at the end of the day, they had both earned enough chips for a blue one, and they drew cards that said "Fro-Yo!" I was the best dad EVER! Total cost for childcare that day? $10.00. All day daycare would have been $80.00 to $100.00.

By the third day, my daughter was harassing me for not working enough so they could earn chips. Bonus!

And they certainly didn't keep track of my time. They just wanted to know that chips were going into the box. How did I count the chips? I gave myself two reds for every unit of GWT, which was 1,000 words or about an hour of work time.

The important thing about GWT is that it doesn't have to be "writing" time. It can be editing time. It can be email time. It can be web design time. It can be social media marketing time. It is a unit of time that you spend on your career. Most of them should be devoted to writing, but a unit is a unit, and you can spend it anyway you like. But it is VITALLY IMPORTANT that you assign an activity to that unit of GWT. If you tell yourself that you're going to spend an hour on the computer doing "important things," and not identify explicitly what those things are, do you know what is going to happen? You're going to spend the hour getting lost in a Wikipedia rabbit hole and get nothing done.

Get a timer. Assign a task to the GWT. ONLY DO THAT TASK for the duration of the GWT.

I'm going to say this again: *you can only do one thing at a time when you are working on a to-do list*. A unit of GWT can only be used to clear ONE line item from your list. If your time is valuable and incrementally stolen from your very busy life, then let yourself focus on one task at a time.

When we're busy in our busy lives, all of the writer life goals seem impossibly out of reach because we don't have the time to get all the necessary tasks done, and this is the sort of thing that makes us freak out a little. It adds stress, which is exactly what we need more of, right? And more stress leads to more overthinking and huffing into a paper bag and wringing our hands and cat vacuuming and . . . and . . . and!

It's all nonsense that you are letting get the better of you because your butt is not in your chair and you aren't typing.

I have a little sheet with nine empty boxes on it. In the morning, I sit down and I write an activity in each of these boxes. "Email," "Website content," "House work," "Errands"—whatever it is that I'd like to accomplish that day that isn't writing. In the rest of the boxes, I write "Make the Words!" This is my GWT chart for the day. Maybe these are hour-long boxes. Maybe they are half hour boxes. It doesn't matter. When I am in one of those boxes, that's the only thing I am working on. I can't leave the box until the task is done, and when it is, I get to cross that box off. At any point in the day, I can look at my sheet and see exactly how productive I've been.

Many of my projects can't be completed in one unit of GWT. I don't scrawl "write book" in one box, and then get furious when it's not done in an hour. I check my magic chart to see where I'm at in the book, and then I write "half of Chapter Six," or "that stupid scene that is dogging me in Chapter 11." And for any other project that I'm working on, I break that project down into line items that can reasonably fit in one unit of GWT.

- Copy edit 10 pages of a manuscript.
- Research the comps for an upcoming title, and fill out the fields in the distributor's intake system.
- Build the front/back matter bookmap for a title.
- Write half a chapter.
- Mow the lawn.
- Make chili for dinner.
- Do two loads of laundry.

I try to assign writing time to at least half the boxes, and when I'm ready to start the day's boxes, I do one or two writing boxes first. Then I take a break, and do one or two of the other boxes. Then, another box of writing, and then a few other boxes. If I clear them all quickly, then I get that last box of writing in—and I leave that one open-ended. I can write and write and write and write. Why? Because I've filled in eight other boxes—I've earned the equivalent of eight red poker chips.

Sure, I bought a lot of frozen yogurt that summer, but I got words done.

EXERCISE

Get a blank sheet of paper. Tear it half so that you have two pieces that are 8.5" tall by 5.5" wide. Draw three rows of three boxes on each sheet. You will notice there is not a lot of space on the page for anything else. This is on purpose. Label one sheet "Tomorrow" and the other one "The Day After." Fill out the nine boxes on each with nine things that you would like to accomplish in your GWT sessions over the next two days.

Check off the boxes as you accomplish these things on these two days.

Give yourself a reasonable self-assessment at the end of the second day on how you did. Adjust your definition of a unit of GWT, if necessary.

Get another sheet of paper. Do this exercise again.

Repeat until the book is complete. Easy peasy lemon squeezy.

THE PARETO PEP TALK

Once upon a time, there was an Italian economist and philosopher who, while standing out on the back porch of his villa, surmised that there was an uneven distribution of peas in the pea pods in his garden. He may have been talking metaphorically about the state of land ownership in Italy; he may have been talking about peas. This is one of those stories where it's best to not get tied up in the minutiae. Having reached this conclusion, he sent workers out into his garden and —lo and behold!— they discovered 20% of his pea pods contained 80% of the peas in the garden. This revelation became known as the Pareto Principle, or more commonly, the 80/20 rule.

20% will produce 80% (and, inversely, 80% will produce 20%), which is to say that 20% of the effort required will produce 80% of the work needed, and that remaining 20% will require 80% of the remaining effort. Basically, you can expend 20% of your energy and net yourself a B grade. Getting that A? That's a lot more work, and the return on that work isn't all that much.

How does this apply to writing? It is the underlying rule to the maxim that "A good book is one that is finished." And by "finished," I mean "you have written a long string of words that ends with 'THE END." Polishing that book? Editing the life out of that book? You're in that remaining 80 for 20 stage. I'm not advocating a lack of editing. More that you should recognize that the bulk of the work is done when you get the words on the page, and it never takes as much effort as you think it does. You should certainly allocate 100% of the effort you think is necessary, but once you get started, the book will happen fairly quickly.

If it doesn't—and this is where you need to have a stern talk with yourself—then what is off-kilter with your plan? The characters are on the page. You have a plot outline. You have filled out all the fields on our master chart. The words should spill out of you, flowing faster than you can type or write. Is there something awry with the plot? Are the characters pushing back against the plan you have? Are you concerned that someone—somewhere—will take offense to your story and talk meanly about your words? Are you worried that this book won't be as "good" as your last book? Or that your book won't be as well received as a similar book written by one of your peers?

Well, these first two concerns can be addressed by taking some time and going back over your planning materials. If you don't want to write the book, there's probably a really simple reason why this is the case, and it will undoubtedly have something to do with the shape of the plot or the characters. You have the power to fix that. You're the writer.

I recently had a conversation with a writer who was struggling with their book. They had a solid plot outline but didn't like the characters. They weren't engaging with the plot like they were supposed to. "Do you know which one is the protagonist?" I asked. They nodded, and I said "So, kill that person in the next chapter, and then write the rest of the book."

They didn't like that suggestion. "But what about all the words that I've done already?"

"It's just words," I said. "You can write more."

"But I . . . I like this character."

"Do you? Because if you did, they'd like you back, and you two would be playing well together. And if that is the case, then maybe that protagonist is pushing back because they're the wrong protagonist for the plot you've got."

I didn't actually think that whacking the protagonist was the solution, but I wanted to shake this writer out of the box they had trapped themselves in. I wanted to give them permission to look hard at the pieces they had collected for the book and seriously question if these pieces were really meant for this book. And if the writer could convince me that everything were it was supposed to be, they would probably realize what wasn't working.

You have to trust that you know—even subconsciously—how to tell a story. And when the story doesn't come, it's because something is not right, and your brain knows that. It may not be able to tell you in a way that you can readily hear (or want to hear), but it is trying nonetheless. And thinking outside the box you've made— talking about the box you've made—is usually enough to let your brain be heard.

As for the remaining concerns, these are completely out of your control. Theodore Sturgeon had a revelation that was later codified into a law, and it is "Ninety percent of anything is crap."[31] This is quintuplely true for commentary on the internet. The best thing you can do for your sanity, your career, and for everyone around you

---

[31] It's in the OED, so it must be true.

is to ignore what anyone says on the internet.

No good ever—EVER—came from trying to correct some jackass's misread of your work. They're just expressing their opinion, which is fine. That's what why we evolved fingers and mouths, though many should probably stick with using those fingers to shove root vegetables and rocks into their mouths, rather than attempt to communicate with electronic signals shot into the intertubes.

If you find yourself unable to step away from the keyboard, here is what I recommend:

- Write a reply that says: "I wrote a book, and you didn't. Hahahahaha!"
- Read it out loud in the privacy of your own space.
- Delete your reply without actually sending it.
- Get on with your life.

That sentence—"I wrote a book, and you didn't"—is all that matters. It's what is pissing them off, and it's what they can't take away from you, no matter how hard they try. You put your butt in your chair, and you made a book. They were busy being outraged on the internet.

Guess which one readers will pay money for?

PART TWO

PLOTTING

WE ARE ALL TREE FARMERS

If the previous section was all about the root structure of your novel, then this section is going to focus on what grows from the rich and fecund soil that you've planted and carefully fertilized. Novels are like topiaries, small trees that have been sculpted from natural materials into specific shapes as imagined by their creators.[32] If a novel is allowed to grow out of control, the branches become all gnarled and tangled. Before you know it, there's a squirrel living in the trunk, and those damn kids are carving their initials in the bark. You want a tree that grows within the boundaries that you set for it, that grows tall and straight, with a heavy canopy of broad leaves that provide shade

---

[32] But more like balloon animals than the twisted topiaries from the Overlook Hotel, right?

year round. You want people to gather beneath your tree and marvel at its thick trunk and hearty branches.

Anyway, the book needs some shaping. It needs strict attention to ensure that it doesn't start sending out tendrils to other books. And it needs to draw sustenance from the roots you have grown within the soil. Our chart is well filled out, and you've probably drawn a circle diagram. It's time to put all this planning to use.

So, let's imagine our tree. It starts out from a tiny nut, a single point from which the rest of the structure will grow. This is our foundation, our world-building nut. Is it healthy? Is it fully formed? Of course, you don't have to know every minute detail of your world, but know enough to make informed decisions about your characters and how they react to stimuli within the world. Of course, it is easy to get lost in world-building. It's fun, after all, but try to restrict yourself to just enough data to feel confident that you know how the world works. Reduce it down to a note that only you're going to read. It's "steampunk with giant bears," or "it's the Wild West with zombies," or "it's New York City in the 1950s, but in a world where WWII never happened."

I used to do a lot of research before I started. Well, I bought a lot of books that I intended to read for research, but I rarely got around to most of them. Partly because I'm lazy, but also because as I wrote the book, I discovered that it was going in a different direction or that it wasn't going deep enough into the topic that I needed to read all six thousand pages that I had on the shelf. Nowadays, I try to wait until I'm fairly confident in the direction of the narrative or the shape of a scene before I disappear into the research hole.

Research is an excuse for not writing, after all. Recognize it for what it is, and treat it accordingly.

Atop that nut of world-building, let's start coaxing out a central trunk. This is narrative foundation that stems from our exploration of the protagonist. Who are they? What external factors are going to shape, influence, or otherwise interact with them? Are there internal factors that will come into play? Who are the other characters, and how are they going to interact with the protagonist? What does the protagonist want? And, in order to fulfill that want, what must the protagonist get? Look at your chart. You can take the list of chapters and start stacking them up, building the trunk of your tree.

And you could keep stacking, but then you're not really making a tree. You're raising a fat stick. We don't want fat sticks for our novels. We want lovely trees with thick branches. Let's give our tree a pair of branches, and because a union is divided when there is a difference within a homogenous body, let's consider these branches to be mirrors of each other. Branches raised in opposition, if you will. Let's call one branch "Unity" and the other, "Separation."

We still have the central trunk, of course, and let's call that "Balance"—a structure equidistant between the two branches.

As our tree grows taller, these branches will split into other branches, and some of these branches will reach back to the trunk, entwine with it, and perhaps even stretch out a leaf or two to the other branch. We're making pathways among our branches now. This will create a fuller canopy of leaves, allowing the topiary shape of the tree to be more finely pruned.

And so where the branches from each branch touch the central trunk again, let's call that "Harmony." At some point in your novel, possibly just after the first act, we're going to have a moment where events and characters come together, and everything seems all rosy and stable. This won't last, of course, but let's not forgo the moment where we embrace the stability of this central trunk.[33]

The other branches continue to grow as well. UNITY remains constant, and if we're building off constancy, then let's mark a point a little farther up that trunk as "Extension." On *SEPARATION*, matters aren't going as well, even though the tree is continuing to grow, and so we'll mark the mirror point on this trunk as "Limitation."

More growth happens. We're closing in on the third act, and offshoots cross back and forth. Near the end of the second act, the protagonist has been through the crucible of transformation, wherein they've assimilated the knowledge they've gained over the course of the narrative (we'll even label a point somewhere there in the middle as such). And then, as we pass into the third act, we mark two more points on the branches—"Action" and "Creation"—before all the branches and the central trunk converge once more at a point we'll label as "Resolution." At this point, your tree diagram may look something like the diagram on the following page.

---

[33] Chapter-wise, this is somewhere just shy of halfway. Typically, I write "Sex" in the chapter description when I'm doing the quick chapter rundown. Laugh all you like, but you'll see that this is the chapter where funny stuff happens. And, of course, the next chapter is "Things Get Worse," because they typically do after sex at this point in the narrative.

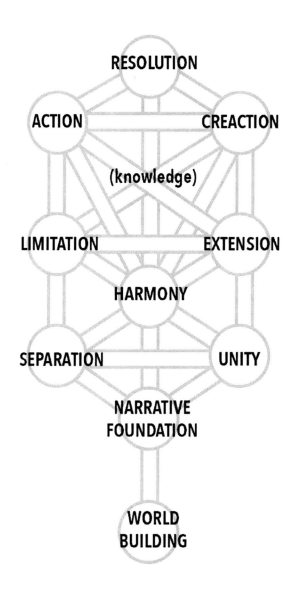

CONNECTING THE PLOT DOTS

Plotting is merely a sequence of events that happen—one after the other—that connect the disparate elements of the narrative arc. Sure, a list of chapters is handy to know the shape of the arc, but the actual procession of events the beginning to the end may still be very . . . questionable. You can fudge it for awhile, but eventually you're going to have to sit down and chart the whole book out. It sounds like work, and it probably is, but you've got a chart, a circle, and now a tree map.

But what is this tree map we just drew? Sure, it looks suspiciously like the Cabalistic Tree of Life, but what does ancient mysticism have to do with writing a book? The same thing as all those mythic foundations to narrative that we discussed earlier, really. This tree and all of its branches are the pathways along which you can plot your book. Each point on this tree leads to other points, and each time you leave a point, you must have another point in mind. And if you pass through a second point on the way to your primary destination, that has an effect within your narrative as well.

Star Wars, for example, starts with Luke Skywalker on Tatooine with some WORLD-BUILDING. And then we get a little NARRATIVE FOUNDATION (the Empire wants stolen plans that are hidden in the brain box of a rogue robot), after which events begin to happen. Luke finds the 'droids, meets Ben Kenobi, and leaves the planet (UNITY).

Alternately, the stormtroopers lose the data and are unable to find the 'droids before they escape the planet (SEPARATION). Meanwhile, Grand Moff Tarkin, feigning lack of concern about the loss of the plans, demonstrates the power of the fully operational battle station on Princess Leia's home planet (EXTENSION). Luke and Ben make new friends (HARMONY), but they are captured by the Death Star before they can get the plans to the rebel alliance (LIMITATION).

All is not lost, as they manage to rescue the princess and escape, but as they are escaping, Vader kills Kenobi,[34] which acts to galvanize the team to finish the mission and deliver the plans to the rebels. The Death Star pursues them (ACTION), and they come up with a working plan to destroy the Death Star (CREATION, also consider this as a REACTION to the ACTION of the other branch), which leads to the final showdown and destruction of the Death Star (RESOLUTION).

Even though we have been focused on mapping out the narrative arc of a protagonist, there is also the matter of the adversary to consider. They are, quite honestly, the protagonist of their own narrative arc, which simply happens to be in utter opposition to the other character's arc. The simplest way to blend these two together is to think of the adversary's narrative as always being on the opposite branch from the protagonist at any given point

---

[34] For the esoteric nerds out there, the spot marked "knowledge" on the tree is known as Da'at, which can be read as either the infinite revelation of the Divine as revealed in the flesh, or the gateway to the Abyss where the seeker is confronted by the possibility of all realities (cf., the Moon in the Tarot).

on the tree.[35] You can use the pathways to move back and forth between the points as you progress through your narrative, but each time you stop, the adversary stops too. Each success of the protagonist is a failure for the adversary, and each failure of the protagonist is an opportunity for the adversary to gloat theatrically and monologue endlessly.

Your narrative structure should move back and forth between both branches of the tree. If it doesn't, you may be writing a fatalistic 19th-century Russian drama about the futility of existence, and while that's probably a crackling good read for when you're in full body traction for a month or two, it's not the sort of book we're working on here. So, set aside your inner Dostoyevsky, and let's keep the narrative moving back and forth across the branches of the tree.

Plotting is linear. You go from point to point to point to point. All this talk of trees and branches is to give you tools to use as you move from point to point. Sure, you can write a book that goes from world-building to narrative foundation to resolution, but—hang on, let me just write that one right now.

Once upon a time there was a family of goats. They all lived in a beautiful valley filled with tall grasses and leafy trees. They ate the grasses and slept under the trees, living happy, long lives. The end.

---

[35] And not only is it critical to consider the adversary as the protagonist of their own arc, but you must treat their arc with the same respect as the protagonist's. Make sure their actions and reactions follow a logical progression of striving to achieve their own goal. Adversaries aren't idiots; they're merely not as clever as the protagonist. Which is to say: their plans would have worked if it hadn't been for those meddling kids . . .

You book should be longer. Therefore, it is going to need to hit a few more plot points.

Back in the day, there was a man named William Wallace Cook who was an even more prolific pulp writer than Lester Dent. Unlike Dent, who devised the fairly straight-forward Master Plot Outline, Cook devised a dizzyingly complex master plot matrix that he called *Plotto*. It starts with a fairly basic theory—"Purpose, opposed by Obstacle, yields Conflict"—but once you get into the minutiae of the opposition part, Plotto turns into a rabbit hole of available paths from A to B to C (almost 1,500, in fact). Cook wrote 40,000 word dime novels that were all sixteen chapters long (and each chapter was exactly five pages of single-spaced type). This is the model of a man who has a plan. You can have one too.[36]

EXERCISE

Map your narrative arc to the tree diagram. Start at a high level and assign a critical chapter to enough of the points that you can follow a path up the tree. Imagine that everything between NARRATIVE FOUNDATION and the pair of ACTION and CREATION is your second act. Pick your chapters accordingly.

Can you fit the remaining chapters, in sequence, along the pathways between each of the points that you've picked? Are you bunching too many chapters along one pathway? Are they spread out too far? Do you find yourself wanting to go up and then back down the tree? Is there much crossover between branches as you work the

---

[36] *Plotto* was packaged in a nice hardback edition by Tin House a few years ago, and it's definitely an interesting book to have on your shelf. Though you almost need an advanced degree in mathematics and programming logic in order to decipher the shorthand code that link all the various plot points together.

pathways?

How do all of these questions illuminate your plan and your action chart?

Naturally, make changes as they become evident.

You may find that we're still working at such a high level that you're not seeing the granularity you'd like for each chapter. "Yes, but how do I get from the start of a chapter to the end?" you're wondering. As it so happens, that's what we're going to talk about next when we discuss the structure of a scene.

CHEWING ON THE SCENERY

If a plot is a series of points connected by pathways, then scenes are the stones upon the pathways.[37] Scenes, much like plot points, follow a linear progression. Even if they don't seem linear, they are—in some fashion. Books have a beginning, a middle, and an end. The arrangement of words on the page may not correspond to the beginning, middle, and the end of the story, and that's fine because writers with MFAs have to have outlets, too. Somewhere, there is a map that reads: "this happens, and then this happens, and then this happens . . ." Each word, each scene, and each plot point occurs in the only order

---

[37] Grouped into clusters conveniently called "chapters," naturally.

possible for the book to have the effect the author wants on the reader's mind.[38]

We know what a plot is, and we know what words are, so what is a scene? A scene is drama, and drama, as screenwriter David Mamet once remarked in a legendary memo to the writers of the television show *The Unit*, is "the quest of the hero to overcome those things which prevent him from achieving a specific, acute goal."[39] A scene, Mamet goes on to explain, must answer three questions:

1) Who wants what?
2) What happens if they don't get it?
3) Why now?

WHO	WANTS	WHAT
HOW	WHY	HOW
WHAT	WHY	HOW

---

[38] Unless you're writing hypertext or some such nonsense, in which case you're on your own. And I say that with great fondness for these sorts of constructions.

[39] http://goo.gl/W6OKyc

Let's break these questions down into a series of discrete boxes.

The first line is simply a reiteration of the first question: "Who wants what?"

The second line asks "How are they going to get it? Why do they want it? And how are they going to be thwarted?"

Finally, the third line is "What is their course of action to get what they want? Why is that quest going to fail? How is it going to fail?" This is your basic breakdown of a scene.

Each of these is boxes is a discrete component of the scene, and if you work through these row by row, you will present information to the reader in a manner that they will naturally absorb. Anytime you find yourself presenting the "WHY" on the second row before you've presented all of the first row, you're probably writing the scene backwards. You're giving us information about the scene prior to us knowing how to position it in relation to the rest of the scene.

Scenes are chunks of information, frankly, delivered in a manner that is dramatic and engaging. We have to pass a lot of information on to the readers so that they understand what is at stake in a given scene, but as soon as they spot us spoon-feeding them this data, they're going to knock the spoon out of our hands and wander off. You have to keep them interested in the spoon. You want them to want the spoon, and you want to give them a way to get the spoon. Does this sound familiar?

What does the person in this scene *want*?

How do they *get* it?

What do they *need* it for?

How will they *use* it?

"Chewing on the scenery" is a phrase used to describe

actors who dive into their roles with such relish that they overplay the emotional content of a scene. Their angst is just shy of offing themselves with every line of dialogue, their outrage is nearly incendiary, and their despair is filled with much gnashing of teeth and tearing of the hair. They're playing like they're doing live theater at an outdoor sports arena, and they want to be sure that the kids in the cheap seats who are a half a mile away can still see the emotional *drama* of the scene. Which gets a little overwrought when an extreme close-up goes up on the Jumbotron.

But you have to think about each scene in your book with this level of intensity. It probably won't make it to the page, but ask yourself exaggerated questions about the scene as you consider it. Who will die if Person A doesn't tell Person B about the ham sandwich in the refrigerator? Will Person C be left alone *forever* if they don't confess their undying adoration for Person D in this scene? Will everyone within a hundred miles be turned into chicken nuggets if Person E doesn't figure out the code to the wall safe in fewer than four seconds?

Most of the time your answer will be in the negative, but in stating as much, you should be able to explain why that scene is important anyway. And if you can't, then what is that scene doing in the book? Or are your characters doing what author John Hedtke refers to as "walking the mall?"[40]

Rajesh Setty wrote an article for Lateral Action about the six levels of engagement in online conversation.[41] In his article, the people conversing start with mindless

---

[40] "Walking the mall" works for Richard Linklater and David Mamet (and for Kevin Smith, to some extent). The rest of us need to have something happen on the page.

[41] http://lateralaction.com/articles/engagement-conversations/

chatter, and then move through successively more direct and personalized levels of interaction until they're actually communicating at a high degree of creative thinking. I once had a customer wander into the bookstore I was working at, and tell me about the six stages of interaction that are embedded in Eric Berne's theories regarding Transactional Analysis.[42] Both of these analyses of communication follow a similar arc.

i. Greeting. Initiating a conversation. *"Hi, how are you?" "I'm fine. How are you?"*

ii. Polite discourse concerning local phenomena. *"Nice weather we're having." "Yes, it's fabulous how lemon-colored the sky is these days."*

iii. Discourse concerning the personal sphere of each individual. *"How are the kids?" "How's your health?"*

iv. Future-looking discourse. *"Any plans for the weekend?" "Still thinking about getting shot into space?"*

v. Critical inquiry and/or revelation of personal information. *"I think I'm turning into a wombat."*

vi. Reaction to revelation or response to critical inquiry. *"Wow. I didn't know about the bees living in your skull. Okay, well, gotta run!"*

---

[42] Naturally, I couldn't find an exact correlation in Berne's work, so take the source of this theory with a grain of salt.

Setty argues that the first three stages require little effort for creative thinking and that they aren't terribly intelligent levels of communication. Polite questions. Polite answers. Everyone is working through their mental list of questions and answers via their mental dropdown lists.[43]

Once we get to layer iv, however, we start asking questions that require some creativity, and then layer v occurs when familiarity between the parties is established, and we can comfortably share actual emotion-rich content. For men, this is the layer where they are prone to panic and flight. For women, this is the layer where they relax and actually communicate. Funny how we're all wired. And then in layer vi, we have the response to the interaction in layer v.

Communication through these six layers is not unlike the structure of a scene. Who wants what? How do they get it? Are they successful, and if so, how do they use what they've received?

As the creative director of this magical gathering, you have to know the purpose of the scene. You have to know what each character wants from that conversation (and many times, what they want is not immediately relevant in the words that are coming out of their mouths).[44]

We're writing long-form fiction, which means we get a little leeway in how we present information to the readers, but each character is living in a world that is scripted not dissimilar to a film or television show. All they get is lines of dialogue. They have to figure out what the other players want from what they say and do. They

---

[43] And let's not forget the classic dropdown menu call and response. "Hey, buddy. You got a dead cat in there, or what?"
"Fuck you, asshole."

[44] cf. any scene in *Downton Abbey*, except for the scenes with the Dowager Countess of Grantham, which are as refreshing as they are bracing for their brash directness.

don't get the luxury of third party omniscient viewpoint.

In fact, screenplay writing will—very quickly—show you whether you are writing around the dialogue or to the dialogue. Adverbs are a sure sign that you're having to explain the emotional emphasis behind a line of dialogue. Pay attention to how your characters are communicating (or not) with each other, and ask yourself why they're not going to the conversational level that you want them to.

As cliché as it is, don't be afraid to ask what any character's motivation is for that—or any—scene.

PRUNING, SHAPING, AND OTHER POLITE WORDS FOR 'CUTTING'

Writing isn't just a matter of stringing words together. Sometimes, you have to unstring the words you've got and restring them. Or get a different string entirely. Hemingway was interested in telling a story; Joyce was interested in having a love affair with language. They're just different writers, approaching their content in different ways. Write in the style of the story that you're telling, but be succinct and to the point. Elmore Leonard's tenth tip for writers is "leave out the parts that readers tend to skip."

I can be terrible at listening to my own advice, and I've been wrestling with the opening of a new novel during the time that I've been drafting this book. And I finally realized that the first ten pages of the book are nothing more than me nattering on about world-building. I'm just getting a feeling for the character and the world he is wandering through. The first line of the book is actually the last line of chapter one because that is where things actually start happening.

First lines are important. Here's a few that I can remember off the top of my head.

The first line of Stephen King's *The Gunslinger* is: "The man in black fled across the desert, and the gunslinger followed."

From *The Rainy City*, the first book in Earl Emerson's Thomas Black series: "On Saturday some ghoul murdered my dog."

From James Joyce's *Finnegan's Wake*: "riverrun, past Eve and Adam's, from swerve of shore to bend of bay, brings us by a commodious vicus of recirculation back to Howth Castle and Environs."

However, can I remember the first line of Stephen King's *Bag of Bones*? Nope. But do I remember the ghost who grabs the protagonist from under the bed at the end of chapter one, thereby hooking me for the rest of the book? Absolutely. Would that moment have worked as well as the first line of the novel? Probably not. Pace yourself. Give the book some room to breathe, but don't give it too much.

My publisher called me after I turned in my draft of *Earth Thirst*, my eco-thriller novel with vampires. My publisher never calls about a book before it comes out. That's not how it worked. But he was taking a vested interest in the titles that year, and he called because he had some notes. Well, one note, really. "Yeah, there's this section where the characters are in Santiago," he said to me. "It just, well, it just drags."

"I know," I said. "I had no idea what happened next and so I was writing until the plot showed up. I was kind of hoping you wouldn't notice, in which case I wouldn't have to fix it."

He laughed and laughed and laughed. "So, you've got this, then?"

"Yep, I got it."

He was talking about a ten-thousand word chunk in the middle. He called because he was worried that I wouldn't react well to having to rework a sizeable chunk of the story. I wasn't worried, because I already knew that not only was that 10K suspect, so was the 15K leading into it. And so I cut them all, reworked the middle, and sent it back.

Ten years before that, I would have tried to rewrite the whole book. But I have learned a few things over time.

I used to loathe editing. Now, it's the point in the writing process that I like best, because it's during this time that I actually feel like I've got a real book on my hands.

Some people write thirty thousand word outlines, and then do one draft of a book and they're done. If I'm going to write 30K, I'm might as well just write the book. Honestly, though? I probably write and cut about 30 - 40K, so it's probably the same amount of work in the end. One of us is more efficient than the other.

And it's important to give yourself permission to cut. Cut dialogue. Cut scenes. Cut subplots. Cut entire character arcs. Be ruthless and mean, and learn to be efficient. Because—and it took some time for this to sink in for me—this is not the only book you're ever going to write. This idea is not your only idea. These lines of dialogue are not the last lines of dialogue that are every going to come out of your fingers. You are a writer. You can always write more words.

The trick, as with everything, is knowing when not to write.

PART THREE

PROGRESS

FALLING DOWN THE WELL (AKA PEP TALK #454)

Here's a familiar scenario: it's the middle of the night, and I've been lying in bed for an hour. I never lie in bed, especially when it is darker than dark outside. Is this "insomnia"? I think it is. It's not something that happens to me, yet, here I am, staring at the ceiling, which I can't see because it's totes dark.

I get up, and turn on my computer, and oh! joy! It wants to update everything. It's not dark anymore, but now I'm just sitting here, staring at my computer screen instead of the ceiling. This is totally calming the crawling sensation of utter helplessness that is working its way under and through and all over my skin. Yep, I'm just supposed to sit here—with all the patience of a saint—and not dwell on all the things that I'm not doing. Not think about all the deadlines that I know are coming. And try really hard not to think about all the ways in which I'm not earning enough money to make ends meet right now.

Brains really suck sometimes.

Mostly, they're helpful, like when you're trying to figure out the best line to use when you're meeting someone you've had your eye on for some months. Or the best response to a cutting remark from a coworker, who you know is just being an ass because they're terrified that they're going to be the one who is going to get cut during the next seasonal Reduction In Force. Or when trying to figure out which of the two windows at the drive-up espresso shack is going to move faster.[45]

And then there are the times when they are nothing but deep dark wells of self-doubt. Especially in the middle of the night. Kind of like your bladder. It needs to be emptied regularly or it starts exerting an awkward pressure on the rest of your internal organs—a rather insistently awkward pressure. Sure, you'd rather be lying there in bed, lolling about peacefully, but oh no, not your bladder. It's full of stuff that it wants to squirt out of your body. And really, wouldn't it be more efficient if you could just evaporate your pee through tiny flaps rather than having to get up, find the toilet, do your business, and stagger back to bed? You could just roll over slightly to make sure your waste vents were not being blocked and *voila!* Urine evaporation.

We should totally get working on this, evolutionarily speaking. Especially if we can do this for doubt. Just roll

---

[45] Neither of which are open at 3am, by the way, when you've finally decided to quit pretending you're going to go back to sleep.

over slightly, expose some brain vents, and *voila!* All our doubts turns to vapor and drift away.

This is the kind of stuff that crosses my mind while I'm waiting for my computer to get done with its business.

Which doesn't entirely drown out the rest of the noise going on in my head. *I'm not writing enough. I'm not doing enough social media. Does the cat like me? Why am I not getting any reviews for my books? Why do these two characters refuse to play well together? How can I make myself look sexier to a prospective agent/editor/publisher? Should I wear a hat in my author photos? Does it make my head look big? Who am I kidding about this writing thing? They're going to spot me for being a phony as soon as I get out of bed, aren't they?*

And on and on. Throw in some financial concerns and a couple dashes of relationship angst and you've got the makings of full-on panic. Maybe someone close to you is dying? That's always good for more unexpected complications in your life. And the cherry on top might be a reduction in hours at your job.

All this. Weighing on you. At two in the morning. When you should be sleeping. When you should be getting the rest your brain needs to produce good, clever content.[46]

This is the deep well of doubt. We all have one—personalized, built by our own our hands, made just for us. We fall into the well more readily when it is dark and we can't see where we're going.[47] Plus it moves around when we're not looking. On occasion, we can throw some boards over it and dance across the top like we're without a care in the world, but eventually, those boards get knocked

---

[46] Of course, two hours later, when I'm writing this chapter, my body tries to insist that I go back to sleep. Thanks for coordinating efforts, body and brain. You two are the best!

[47] Sometimes metaphors are more real than you want them to be.

aside, and the hole starts gaping at us again. Big and dark. Waiting for us.

There's probably a dead fish or two down there. Shouldn't we go check?

Here's a secret: no one else can see this hole that follows you around. No one else is going to accidentally fall into your well of doubt. You made it up, and you can un-make it up. If you're lying in bed at two in the morning, get up. Go sit on the toilet, take a deep breath, and let all of this fear and apprehension out. You don't have doubt vents any more than you have urine vents, and the only way to get all of this terror out of you is to forcefully—mindfully—expel it. Sit and piss it away, if you like. It's just waste that needs to be dumped. *Fear is the mindkiller*, goes the old saying,[48] and who cares if it comes from a book about some desert planet far in our future. It's still true.

Fear keeps you awake. Fear keeps you from making a choice. Fear keeps you from daring to do something different and amazing. Fear keeps you from realizing that you've got this.

We're writers. We play the *What if?* game more often and more readily than small dogs think about break-fast. Doubt is nothing more than your brain sputtering through all the permutations and scenarios that you've been throwing in your own path. Once it runs out of those, what is it going to do? It's going to get in trouble because it doesn't have anything better to do. It's absolutely responsible and forward-thinking of you to consider all the possibilities, but once you've done a round or two of

---

[48] One of the more memorable Bene Gesserit sayings from *Dune*, and I'm willing to bet it started out as a bit of marginalia that Frank Herbert wrote to himself as he was wondering if this whole ecological-SF-desert-world, giant-sandworms book was a good idea.

mental extrapolation, stop. Move on.

As with all things in life and in fiction, once you stop endlessly circling the dark well of doubt, you'll start moving forward again. And you know what? Just as your characters experience obstacles and opportunities in their second act, so will you. Embrace them or dodge them. Be as clever as your characters. Why? Because you invented them, and anything they can do, you can do as well. Make choices that will either close doors or open new ones, because that is what you do when you climb out of the well and start moving forward.

Lying in bed at two in the morning, waiting for your bladder to fill, is floating around at the bottom of the well. Climb out, pee (if you need to), and go make something. A sandwich, a cup of tea, a blanket fort. It doesn't matter. It's not floating. It's moving.

KEYBOARD TRIUMPHANT

Look. Writing is work. It can be easy work or it can be hard work, but it is still work, nonetheless. It may look like you're not doing much when you're sitting there with your feet up on the desk, staring at the ceiling. Or when you're off vacuuming the cat for the fortieth time this week. And you certainly don't build muscles writing like you do when you're out working construction. Nor do you get any sort of decent tan.

What we do have is charts and graphs and diagrams that tell a story. All that is left to do is put some words down. Lovely, lovely words. And the only way those words are going to happen is if you put your butt in your chair and your fingers on your keyboard. Eighty percent of why you don't write is an excuse, which is fine, really, because we know that the other twenty percent is totes sweet productive time, don't we? That's when all the writing happens anyway, right?

Heck, I just wasted the first hour of my two hour writing block this morning when I should have been working on this chapter. Why? Because I was staring at a blank page, and I didn't have a snappy anecdote to start things off (read excuse). I had a pretty good idea of what I wanted to say in this chapter, but I didn't know how I was going to say it, and so I didn't. I fiddled around the office, paid some bills, and stared out the window for a bit. And now, I've only got an hour today instead of two. I'm going to type faster in this hour to make up for not working. It's a terrible way to be productive, but it's my way, more often than not. I own it, though, and at the end of the day, I still get to put a number down in the column for today's word count. I don't bother writing how I got those words. What matters is that I got them.

We talked about units of GWT in the planning section, and how it takes many units of GWT to write a book. If you stare at that number, the project can seem impossible, so don't stare at it. Give yourself a goal you know you can hit. If you think you can get ten units in a week, put a stack of twelve counters in a box on your desk. At the end of every day, open the box and take out however many units you earned. Or put counters in an empty box. Whichever works better for you. The important point is that the box is closed when you're working so that you have no idea how many counters are in there (or not).

It's the same if you use a stopwatch timer for your GWT unit. Don't put it where you can see it counting. It's not Schrödinger's stopwatch. It's counting whether you look at it or not. Let it do its job without you hovering over it. Focus on writing and not clock-watching.

And hey, if you empty your counter box before the end of the week, put some back in and earn them out again. Give yourself a reward, though, for hitting your goal. If it is a good reward, it's worth trying to hit twice in a week.

In the video game world, this is called the "feedback loop." All modern games have many, many micro goals that stack up while you're trying to reach whatever primary goal state there is for the game. Most games have between forty and a hundred million hours of gameplay built into them. If we had to play the minimum before we got any sort of reward, no one would finish a game. But there are many minor goals that can be achieved on the way. "Log in four days in a row, and get a fox hat." "Stab fifty orcs, and get double XP for the rest of the week."

These are all little things that keep you playing. "Oh, I've killed forty-two orcs today. Well, I guess I can keep playing for another hour to stab those last eight . . ."

Build feedback loops for your writing time. If you use poker chips for your counters, create goal states for the colored chips. Blues are worth five hundred words. Five blues gets you a green. Green chips can be turned in for a visit to the frozen yogurt shop. Ah, but five green chips can be turned in for a red chip, which can be redeemed for a visit to the local bookstore or a movie night.

Use the chips for the whole family. You earn a red chip, which is worth having someone else cook you dinner some night. But aha! Your partner has earned two red chips by taking care of other household chores while you've been writing, and they trump you with "What me, cook? We're going out!" reward.

Feedback loops—these micro goals—work when it is possible to earn them quickly and regularly. You should be able to earn at least one or two counters for every unit of GWT. Nothing makes your day run more smoothly than you being obnoxiously pleased with yourself for having done a productive amount of creative work. Conversely, nothing sucks the fun out of the room faster than a writer sulking about how deep they've fallen into the well of doubt.

A writer friend of mine once struggled with getting his butt in his office chair. He liked writing; he just didn't like sitting in that room. And so, he plastered the walls of the room with centerfolds from various magazines, and shockingly! he didn't mind being in that room as much anymore.

Some writers write at a desk that faces a blank wall so that they aren't distracted. For awhile, I had to write at a noisy coffee shop with my headphones blaring loops of rhythmic noise because that was the only way I could shut everything out enough to focus on the page.[49]

Progress happens because work gets done. At the end of the day, you want to run up the Keyboard Triumphant banner, so that everyone knows that you've been productive. It's not a subjective act—the raising of the banner—it's either up or down. Did you make words? Then the banner goes up.

Writing is writing, except when it is editing, and you can't edit anything until you've written something.

A good book is a book that is finished.

A better book is one that has been polished and released into the world.

James Joyce once took two days to finish two sentences for Ulysses. When asked if that time had been spending trying to find the right words, Joyce is said to have replied, "No, I have the words already. What I am seeking is the perfect order of words in the sentences I have."

---

[49] I can still write just about anywhere, but I do get fussy about a chair being too soft.

No one is going to love your book as much as you do. Except when you've been through it eight times during editorial, and then, everyone is probably going to like the book more than you do.

And there will be frustrated egomaniacs who will hate your book merely because they're enraged that someone wrote something and they have to pay for the pleasure of hating it. There's not much to be done about those folks.

Many people just won't care one way or another that you wrote a book. These are all reasons for you to pre-judge your book, thereby giving yourself permission to abandon it out in the muddy field behind your house on some moonless night.

Well, if that's what you want . . .

But's that not the narrative arc you've assigned yourself is it? What's the first part of the story of You the Writer? Identifying what you WANT. And what do you want? To go dig a hole out in a muddy field and bury your laptop or your journal or whatever thing it is that is the embodiment of your creative effort? I'm not kidding. Get a shovel. Put it in your hand and ask yourself, "Is this what I'm going to do with my work?"

Look at the icon at the start of this chapter. It's a hand holding a keyboard. Not a shovel. There is no banner for *Buried My Novel*. And even if there was one, no one is going to drop by unexpectedly to share a bottle of decent bourbon with you if you're flying the *Buried My Novel* banner.

So, put the shovel down and pick up the keyboard again. Your neighbors want to come over and drink *with* you. They don't want to sit in their own homes and talk worriedly *about* you while drinking by themselves.

Writing is a solitary practice, but the end result enriches your community. Sure, you can tell yourself that you are writing just for you, but that only works until the book is done. At which point, you've done something for other people. And they'll appreciate it.

Well, the ones that matter will. The rest aren't worth your trouble. They're the one who show up late to parties, who don't bring anything to share, who noisily drink all your booze, and who miss the toilet when they use the bathroom. You don't really want them coming by anyway.

THE DETERMINED OCTOPUS

The thing about octopuses is not that they're able to squeeze themselves through keyholes or undo jar lids from the inside of jars. Nor is it the fact that they're probably alien to this world, sent by some other intelligence to spy on us. No, the thing about octopuses is all those tentacles. And suckers. Which make it easy to hold lots of pens. But lots of pens don't always mean getting more work done.[50]

We've done a lot of drawing and doodling and creating lists in the course of this book, and when you spread it all out on your desk, it can seem like you've got too much to do. It will be tempting to try to do all of the things all at

---

[50] Unless you're an ambidextrous sort like Comte de St. Germain, and even then you've only got two hands.

once. Just like that fellow there in the picture at the top of this chapter. He's got eight arms—three of them with pens. He should be able to do everything.

But he can't even get that first word right.

He's not going to give up, though. Maybe he'll tear off that first page and start over. Maybe he'll get a bottle of white goop and fix that bungled letter. Maybe he'll turn it into abstract art instead of the first page of a script. Whatever his solution, he's moving forward.

Be the determined octopus. Blow a scene when you're drafting the book. Do what I do and write "[WELL, THIS IS ALL MESSED UP, BUT I WANT TO GET TO THE EXPLODY BITS IN THE NEXT CHAPTER AND SO I'LL FIX THIS LATER]." After all, you should give yourself something to edit on the second pass. Otherwise, you'll think that you can draft a finished book in one pass, and that's dangerous thinking, my friend.

When I wrote on the commuter train, I worked in a such a piecemeal fashion that I ended up having the same clever conversation between two characters three times. Clearly, it was an important conversation to have, but only one of those three instances was the right one. Sure, I should have remembered what I was doing a little more readily, but instead of stopping during the drafting process to go look for the conversation, I just kept writing.

Progress happens because you show up. Regularly. If you look at the track record of bestselling authors, you'll find—more often than not—their breakout book isn't their first. Rick Riordan wrote six (or seven) mystery novels for adults before *The Lightning Thief* came out and made him a YA superstar. Suzanne Collins wrote the five books of *The Underland Chronicles* before she landed on *The Hunger Games*. Janet Ivanovich wrote twelve romance novels before she landed on the Stephanie Plum character with *One For the Money*.

Keep writing. The good books are the ones that aren't just in your head any more.

And if you falter or wander astray, remember that you have your notes and all our of exercises. Revisit them. See if you come up with the same scenarios for these exercises as you did the first time. What's changed in the interim? Do you know the characters better? Has the world of your novel drifted too far from where you started with it? How can you get back in sync with it?

If you feel like you've paved a road off into the wilderness and you're far—so very, very far—from where you are supposed to be, don't pull up the road and backtrack. Figure out how to correct your course back to the original plan. It's easier to create a shortcut that runs right through when you've got the beginning and the end connected.

And, in the end, that's what it is: a book is a line. It's a series of events that runs from a beginning, through a middle, to an end. It's a line—it may curve a bit and twist back on itself, but it's still a continuous line. The determined ones keep putting one foot in front of the other. Or, one tentacle in front of the other.

Learn how to fit through keyholes and undo lids from inside jars before you learn how to write with both hands. Those are more useful life skills anyway.

EXEUNT

Recently, I've taken to reading writing books while visiting the bathroom. It's not that I think most of them are crap; it's quite the opposite, in fact. Time on the throne is one of the few moments of the day when I'm not at the liberty of someone else's schedule. What happens in the secret back room happens in its own time, at its own pace.[51] You might as well take a book in there with you. The nice thing about writing books is that many of them are meant to be read piecemeal.

With that in mind, I'd like to offer this final section as the "Bathroom Reading" section, AKA Bullet Points for Bowel Movements.

* How long you write in any one sitting does not matter. Knowing how long that period of time is, and creating a schedule where you get that unit of Glorious Writing Time on a very regular basis is all that matters.

---

[51] If you're fortunate enough (or young enough) that this isn't an issue, then you can skip this final summary. Go get your butt in the chair and write, you damn youngster!

* Someone is always writing faster than you are just as someone is always writing slower than you. *"Are you writing?"* is the only question that is worth asking and answering.

* All plots grow out of a single tiny idea—the small seed you plant in rich, compost-heavy soil. How that seed grows into a tree is up to you, as is how well you tend to your tiny seedling as it grows into a broad, canopied tree.

* The people around you do not want to you to fail. They want you to succeed because they like you better when you're not soggy and wet from having dunked yourself in the well of doubt. They do not know what it is like to be a writer, but they can be thrilled to have one about. Teach them how to properly feed and ignore you. Build your feedback loops.

* "Purpose, opposed by Obstacle, yields Conflict." This is your mantra. Apply it to every scene.

* When in doubt, move sideways. Pull a Tarot card. Use "And then, nuns with guns entered the room." The real question here is Why has your book stopped moving forward?

* Chew on the scenery, and when it is soft and malleable, spit it out. What's left is probably what the scene is really about. Start there.

* All mythic structure is true. It's also a crutch. Use it to guide you back, and let go of it when you know where you are going.

* WANT. GET. NEED. USE. Quarter the circle. Work through it whenever you can. This is the wheel of fortune, and it turns over and over and over again. Ride it.

* A good book is a finished book. Just as a writer is someone who writes. The rest is semantics.

APPENDIX A: EXTRA READING

Writing and the Creative Process

Austin, J. L., *How to Do Things With Words* (Harvard University Press, 1975).

Bradbury, Ray, *Zen in the Art of Writing* (Bantam, 1992).

Chandler, Raymond, *The Simple Art of Murder* (Vintage Crime, 1988)

Cook, William Wallace, *Plotto: The Master Book of All Plots* (Tin House Books, 2011).

Currey, Mason, *Daily Rituals* (Alfred A. Knopf, 2013).

Field, Syd, Screenplay: *The Foundations of Screenwriting* (Delta, 2005).

Fish, Stanley, *How to Write a Sentence And How to Read One* (HarperCollins, 2011).

Goldberg, Natalie, *Writing Down the Bones* (Shambhala, 2005).

King, Stephen, *On Writing* (Scriber, 2010).

Madden, David, *Revising Fiction* (Plume, 1988)

McKee, Robert, *Story: Substance, Structure, Style and the Principles of Screenwriting* (Regan Books, 1997).

Miller, Henry, *On Writing* (New Directions Publishing, 1964)

Rand, Ken, *The 10% Solution* (Fairwood Press, 1998).

Rand, Ken, *From Idea to Story in 90 Seconds* (Fairwood Press, 2007).

Smiley, Jane, *13 Ways of Looking at the Novel* (Anchor Books, 2006).

Truby, John, *The Anatomy of Story: 22 Steps to Becoming a Master Storyteller* (Faber & Faber, 2008).

Vandenburgh, Jane, *Architecture of the Novel* (Counterpoint, 2010).

Wilson, Colin, *The Craft of the Novel* (Ashgrove Press, 1990).

Wood, James, *How Fiction Works* (Picador, 2008).

—, *The World Split Open* (Tin House Books, 2014).

Tarot

Anonymous, *Meditations on the Tarot* (Element, 1985).

Crowley, Aleister, *The Book of Thoth* (Samuel Weiser, 1944).

Greer, Mary K., *21 Ways to Read a Tarot Card* (Llewellyn Publications, 2006).

Jodorowsky, Alejandro & Marianne Costa, *The Way of Tarot* (Destiny Books, 2009).

Katz, Marcus, *Tarosophy* (Salamander and Sons, 2011).

Kenner, Corrine, *Tarot for Writers* (Llewellyn Publications, 2009).

Papus, *The Tarot of the Bohemians* (Arcanum Books, 1962).

Pollack, Rachel, *Seventy-Eight Degrees of Wisdom* (Weiser, 2007).

Pollack, Rachel, *Tarot Wisdom* (Llewellyn Publications, 2011).

Vogler, Christopher, *The Writer's Journey* (Michael Weise Productions, 1992).

Waite, Arthur Edward, *The Pictorial Key to the Tarot* (William Rider and Son, 1911).

Mythology

Campbell, Joseph, *The Hero With a Thousand Faces* (New World Library, 2008).

Campbell, Joseph, *The Masks of God* [in four volumes] (Penguin, 1991).

Eliade, Mircea, *The Myth of the Eternal Return* (Princeton University Press, 2005).

Eliade, Mircea, *The Sacred and the Profane* (Harcourt Brace Jovanovich, 2007).

Jung, Carl Gustav, *Four Archetypes* (Princeton University Press, 1970).

APPENDIX B:
NARRATIVE ARC BY TAROT

Here's an example of using the tarot to build a narrative arc for a protagonist. I like to use a deck that has images that are representative of the genre of the book that I'm planning to write because the art of the cards helps put my creative brain in the right headspace book. Occasionally, after I do one reading, I'll get one or two more decks out and replicate the reading with those decks. Just to put a wide variety of visual magic in front of my eyeballs. Your mileage may vary.

A deck that is rich with symbols and colors is always preferred, and unless you have a specific relationship with one of the more common decks (the Rider-Waite or some version of the Marseille deck), I do recommend picking up a deck that is a little out of your comfort zone (both in images and in understanding of all the symbols). This will force you to dig a little deeper in order to parse the cards.

After taking a moment to clear my head, I deal ten cards in the Celtic Cross layout, and the cards fall in the following order:

1. THE HEART - ACE OF WANDS
2. THE ADVERSARY - QUEEN OF SWORDS
3. THE ROOT - LUST
4. THE PAST - EMPRESS
5. THE VISION - NINE OF SWORDS
6. THE FUTURE - ACE OF SWORDS
7. THE MIRROR - FOUR OF PENTACLES
8. THE EYE - KNIGHT OF WANDS
9. THE GUIDE - TWO OF WANDS
10. THE OUTCOME - THE MOON

Now, before I begin to sort out the narrative arc, I look for patterns in the cards, and already I can see that we've got lots of wands and swords. Wands are the suit of fire, and swords are the suit of air, and air comes about because of a conjunction of fire and water, which sets up a hierarchy of the swords being subservient to the wands—and there's a source of conflict right there. The Queen of Swords is laid across the Ace of Wands, suggesting, again, the adversarial struggle between swords and wands.

There are three Major Arcana cards: Lust (or Strength), the Empress, and the Moon. In the Thoth deck designed by Aleister Crowley (which I used for the first pass at this reading), Strength is renamed to Lust because Crowley believed the card to signify more than just strength; for him, it also signified the joy of strength being exercised. There's a hedonist element to Crowley's Lust (naturally), which suggests dominance in a sexual manner or strength used to control versus strength used to uplift.

The Thoth deck has a wealth of symbolism woven into all of the cards, but many of the interpretations can quickly stray from virtue to vice through over-indulgence. We have Lust for the Root and the Empress for the Past, suggesting that our protagonist has come from a realm that is indulgent in its embrace. A person of money and means, perhaps.

Our outcome is the Moon, which is the threat of over-indulgence realized. The Moon is the threshold of madness, but it is also the gate to radical creativity. This is the gate through which the artist must pass during their transformative arc. The Moon symbolizes the entirety of the passage through the Underworld in the Campbellian interpretation. Whoever our protagonist is, they're going to be launched into darkness.

The Empress is also a gate, so we have passage from one realm into the realm of the immediate story, and then on to the realm beyond the threshold of madness.

Above and in front of the protagonist we have two sword cards—the ace and the nine—matching in opposition the two Major Arcana cards. Both are suggestive of the primordial state of air. In the case of the nine, it is the power of air returning to rest. Disorder is now rectified. Chaos has been calmed. This is the vision—what the protagonist wants. In the immediate future, though, is the purest form of air. It's the state before disorder and chaos, and so the question this card raises is what actions on the part of the protagonist cause a change in the calm order of air so that they seek a return to that state?

Frankly, this is the basic structure of the Hero's Journey: our hero finds their world out of balance, so they leave that heretofore Edenic state and travel through the underworld, seeking the boon that will rescue their world. Once the boon is received, they return, and all is well again. So, it seems like we're setting up a narrative of a journey that is sticking fairly close to the Hero's Journey.

So what have we got along the way? The four of pentacles is the Mirror—the protagonist as they are seen by the world at large. The four of pentacles is usually represented as a quartet of pyramids that protect a precious center. They are law and order, under constant vigilance. Then we have the knight of wands, who is the fiery part of fire, which is both good and bad. He's the guy who will never give up on his mission, but he's not the brightest thinker in the bunch, which means that if his original effort is flawed in some manner, he's got nothing in his saddlebags that is going to save him. He's the guy who will charge off the cliff because it is there and he doesn't know how to turn his horse.

And then we have the two of wands, which is the state of fire after the ace. If the ace is the primordial idea of fire—fire before fire—then the two is that fire given intent. It is the fire that burns and destroys, because before you create you have to separate. You have to destroy something before you have any pieces to work with.

It's a reading that suggests our protagonist is doomed in his quest, or that he's questing for something that is going to turn out to not quite be the boon he thinks it is. The Queen of Swords is gracious and benevolent, but she's also capricious and sly. She's not averse to seducing you to her side, and then sending you off to do her dirty work without telling you that said work involves killing puppies.

Even with all of this, I didn't have a solid idea of who the protagonist was, and so I drew one more card to give me a clearer representation of this individual. I drew the Sun—the Major Arcana card that represents the pure Blakean child—one who has made the journey from innocence to experience and back again. The child who has escaped Philip K. Dick's black iron prison and is ready to emerge into the world again. In Egyptian mythology, this child is Horus, who is born from the union of Osiris, the death and resurrection god, and Isis—the mother goddess figure. Osiris was slain by Set, in one of the age-old wars between the Hero and the Adversary, and Set dismembered Osiris, scattering the pieces of the slain god across the world. Isis gathered them all up,[52] and brought Osiris back to life enough for a child to be conceived. Horus is the man Osiris can no longer be,[53] and it is Horus who sends Set packing.

So, the sun. Or, the son. Depending on how you want to look at it.

Which makes me think of *Hamlet*. And *Oedipus*.

On the deck I'm using, the Queen of Swords is holding a severed head in one hand, and she's got a sword in the other. I think she's slain her husband in order to take the throne for herself. But in whatever world this is, she can't rule without a king, so she seeks a consort who will be malleable and subservient. Enter our protagonist, untested and unproven on the field of battle and in the chambers of love and politics. Is he the queen's son? That's a little twitchy, but what if he is a clone of the dead king? A piece of the old man, grown in a vat under the strict order of the queen. He is poured out into the world (the gate of the empress, if you will), where he must be blooded and tested in order to fully come into his heritage. He is, at the beginning, an idea without form. He comes into the world—did the queen set this plan in motion during sexual congress with her husband?—and wants nothing more than to be the best son/king ever. At

---

[52] Except for his penis, because what's a good bit of world-building without a castration motif to keep the young lads in line?

[53] Which basically translates to "Kids, if you're dead AND missing your junk, you're probably never going to be king again. Give up the crown to someone who has a little more going for them."

this point, he is the ace of swords: perfectly poised to do . . . something.

And so he does. He leaves the safety of his perfect world (the four of pentacles), intent on his mission for his queen (the knight of wands), but somewhere along the way, he becomes clued in to the machinations going on around him. He's like Hamlet who discovers that his mother, the queen, has slain his father, but she doesn't want to put some other dude on the throne, she wants to put him on the throne, because he is a purified version of his father. Yeah for the magic of genetic engineering!

Naturally, this causes our protagonist to go a little bonkers.

This narrative arc is missing the third act, but I can go to Hamlet for that final structure if I still need it when I've gotten to that point in the book. And yes, this does feel like *Hamlet* meets *Oedipus* IN SPACE, but Shakespeare gives us credence to circle around again on ideas in his fifty-ninth sonnet.

> *If there be nothing new, but that which is*
> *Hath been before, how are our brains beguil'd,*
> *Which, labouring for invention, bear amiss*
> *The second burden of a former child.*

What is old is new again in about fifteen years (witness the endless spate of remakes and reboots in television and film), so don't worry too much about leaning on source material. Stories are enriched because they extend back through our cultural and literary heritages. But whatever you do use for foundation stones, make sure you mix the mortar a little differently, because you are different than all the writers who have gone before. You're different than me and that weirdo on the bus and all those marvelous readers out there who are waiting for another book from you.

Be inventive. We use the known structures and the mythological models because they are familiar and our audiences like the comfort of familiarity, but stamp them with your passion and your quirky sense of humor and your passion. Stamp them so very hard with your passion.

ACKNOWLEDGEMENTS

Grateful tip of the hat to the gang who showed up for my Clarion West One-Day Workshop where some of the material for this book was tested. I drew on a white board for a few hours, and they took notes like I was making articulate noises. Hopefully, the arrangement of words in this book more readily present the ideas I was attempting to share that day versus the shaky handwriting and egg-shaped attempts at drawing circles that passed for diagramming during my presentations.

Also, eternal gratitude to Darin Bradley, all around creative guru who took care of my cover, my copy edits, and damn near anything else I want to fret about during the process of producing this book.

Fran Wilde graciously responded to my plea for interior art with her usual aplomb and hilarious illustrations. I strive to make words that are as charming and winsome as her drawings.

Thanks also to Guy Windsor for using the phrase "mystic shit" once upon a time in reference to something else entirely, but I think he'd approve of its use herein.

Extra whiskey rations for both Erica Sage and Evelyn Nicholas, who dealt with writer panics as they should be dealt with, which is to say they parroted back the same pithy aphorisms I had said to them at some point during the last six months. It's cute the first few times; after that, it's kind of annoying to realize you're not listening to your own advice. Good thing they're polite about reminding me.

ABOUT THE AUTHOR

I've been writing most of my life—some of it professional, most of it passionately. I've written thrillers, urban fantasy, erotic romance, historical adventure stories, ghost stories, experimental WTF? projects, comic scripts, movie scripts, and a lot of marketing copy. I've run a transmedia property (*The Foreworld Saga*), which had books, novellas, comics, movie scripts, TV scripts, and game narratives.

I own and operate a small publishing company called Resurrection House, which has a number of imprints for both core genre and the uncertain fringe of genre.

I've edited, rewritten, ghost-written, pitched, made up wild cover copy, nodded sagely at words written by better writers than I, and run group brainstorm sessions that have done and undone an entire season's worth of work in two or three sessions. I wrote five distinct versions of my second novel because I didn't know how to line edit.

I write fewer drafts now.

I'm on the web at markteppo.com. You can find my full CV under the ABOUT section of the website.

My twitter handle is @markteppo.

In this regard, I try to be easy to find.

Beyond that, I am drawn to the symbolism of the Hermit card in the Tarot deck, and I try to spend my non-writing time out discovering new things and digging up forgotten lore.

LEAVING FEEDBACK

If you've found this book to be useful, please consider leaving a review at your favorite online venue (Goodreads, Shelfari, Amazon, Barnes & Noble, et cetera). Reviews and stars mean a lot to independent writers as they are the metric by which they are judged by the all-mighty and all-knowing algorithm. While buying a second copy of this book and giving it to a friend is a delightful and welcome reaction to the words herein, leaving a review and a rating is also greatly appreciated.

Stars = Love.

Shameless, I know. But it's what makes the world go 'round these days.

We can be rebels when it comes to our punctuation, but let's play the game when it comes to showing the love for authors.

And I'm not asking just for myself. Go give some stars to someone else whose book you've loved. Do it. I know it'll feel good.

"Any man who keeps working is not a failure. He may not be a great writer, but if he applies the old-fashioned virtues of hard, constant labor, he'll eventually make some kind of career for himself as a writer."

—Ray Bradbury

CPSIA information can be obtained at www.ICGtesting.com
Printed in the USA
LVOW12s0502020316

477284LV00003B/12/P

9 781630 231002